Prayers
of
Blessing
over My
Adult Children

Bruce Wilkinson

and Heather Hair

HARVEST HOUSE PUBLISHERS
EUGENE, OREGON

Cover design by Rightly Designed

Cover photo © korkeng / Adobe Stock

Interior design by Rockwell Davis

Prayers of Blessing over My Adult Children
Copyright © 2020 by Bruce Wilkinson and Heather Hair
Published by Harvest House Publishers
Eugene, Oregon 97408
www.harvesthousepublishers.com

ISBN 978-0-7369-8007-4 (pbk)
ISBN 978-0-7369-8008-1 (eBook)

Library of Congress Cataloging-in-Publication Data

Names: Wilkinson, Bruce, author. | Hair, Heather, author.
Title: Prayers of blessing over my adult children / Bruce Wilkinson and
    Heather Hair.
Description: Eugene, Oregon : Harvest House Publishers, 2020. | Summary:
    "You expected to lose sleep when your kids were young but thought by the
    time they were on their own, you'd worry less. Use guided prayer to
    approach God with a spirit of praise and boldly pray over your adult
    children and their specific needs"-- Provided by publisher.
Identifiers: LCCN 2020008171 (print) | LCCN 2020008172 (ebook) | ISBN
    9780736980074 (trade paperback) | ISBN 9780736980081 (ebook)
Subjects: LCSH: Parents--Religious life. | Prayer--Christianity. | Prayers.
    | Parent and adult child--Religious aspects--Christianity. |
    Families--Religious aspects--Christianity.
Classification: LCC BV4529 .W5565 2020 (print) | LCC BV4529 (ebook) | DDC
    242/.645--dc23
LC record available at https://lccn.loc.gov/2020008171
LC ebook record available at https://lccn.loc.gov/2020008172

Printed in the United States of America

20 21 22 23 24 25 26 27 28 / BP-RD / 10 9 8 7 6 5 4 3 2 1

Contents

Introduction

Those of us who have adult children often experience great pain as we watch them go through the difficulties that occur in life. Our children and grandchildren face a much more hostile and wicked world than we did as we grew up. They live in a day where truth entangles with lies in an ongoing, ever-present manner. Faith fails when it is no longer rooted and grounded in truth.

If you are a parent of adult children, just picking up this book of prayers may be a major step for you. We realize the whole matter of praying for your children may bring up emotionally painful memories and unresolved issues. So we applaud you for pressing forward to pray for your family. While your role of parent may have shifted as to its expectations when your children entered adulthood, your heart as a parent never changes. Your inner cry to pray for your adult children is a healthy one. Honor that desire and pray regularly for your adult children, even when you do not yet see the answers to those prayers.

Many of the guided prayers in this book have been written to help set you free from some of the common parental traps faced today. But even though some of these prayers may address difficult topics, we want to remind you to end each prayer with hope. Hope in God's promises, mercy, compassion, lovingkindness, and His deep desire for your adult children's best. God is not restricted by the wickedness of society. Rather, He can overpower our adversaries as we dwell beneath His protective wings.

One of the deceitful lies of the enemy is that our adult children's wrong and painful decisions are a result of our parental mistakes and errors. It is our hope that this book will set you free from that lie. Ultimately, God does hold us, as parents, responsible for the decisions and responses we choose to make in our own lives. However, as parents, we are not responsible for the failings of our children. There are many godly parents in the Bible who had rebellious or wicked children. Eli, Samuel, and many of the godly kings of Judah remind us of the fact that God-honoring parents do not always produce God-honoring children.

Sometimes, however, our personal sins will result in our children's rebellion and even betrayal, such as happened with Absalom, the son of King David. Such consequences must be endured by parents of adult children until God has had the opportunity to accomplish all that He desires in the lives involved. Thankfully, everything has a beginning and an end, though at times we must hold on for years or even decades to see God's desired result come to fruition.

Because much of life is beyond our understanding, we cannot allow bitterness to take root when things get difficult with our adult children. Rather, we should realize that everything we face provides us with an opportunity to grow and learn, and we must choose God no matter what comes our way.

Darlene and I (Bruce) just returned from a funeral yesterday. The forty-one-year-old daughter of one of our friends had drunk herself to death—the blood vessels in her esophagus and stomach burst open for the fourth time and all the emergency interventions couldn't save her. What a sobering and sad moment, especially with her two married children sitting in the front row.

Three days ago, I dropped off a check to another friend from church whose twenty-one-year-old son was facing a trial for selling drugs, which will likely result in considerable jail time. Darlene and I sent some money to help with the legal fees.

My wife currently is praying with a pastor's wife on the other side of the country as two of her adult children are doing well, but the third has turned her back on the Lord and all of Christianity. Such tears.

A few weeks ago, we attended a beautiful wedding of another close friend's daughter. She was born again, thankfully, but due to a major church crisis a decade ago that had deeply hurt her parents, she had turned her heart against the Lord. She was marrying a nice young man, but he would have nothing to do with Christ or Christianity. We sat with her parents after the wedding, joy mixed with a great burden.

A month ago, while ministering with some American friends in South Africa, Darlene and I wept with a couple who had adopted two young children from another nation. They loved them, cared for them, and raised them with solid Christian values and teaching. One of them became addicted to drugs and tragically committed suicide just a little while ago.

Another good friend's teenage child was caught stealing a few things from the local Walmart. The child came home and, in a moment of despair, hanged himself in his bedroom.

We could share many more stories, but we are sure you can add your own...

At the same time, we know of families whose adult children are flourishing in their walk with God and their service to Him. They are bright spots of the power of God's redeeming love and restoring grace.

We are so glad you picked up this powerful book. Although you may be a parent with adult children who are walking with the Lord and you enjoy peace and joy regarding their lives, we believe the vast majority of people purchased this book out of a sense of pain, distress, fear, and lingering feelings of parental failure.

Keep in mind that the first section of this book seeks to prepare your mind and heart to pray in a powerful way for your adult children. You'll find the prayers in the next section. Who are we and why did we write this book? Darlene and I (Bruce) have three adult children and ten grandchildren. We also have suffered the loss of a close relative due to an unexpected teen suicide. We are Baby Boomers and have seen firsthand the shift of family and personal values in our culture. Jack and I (Heather) are a blended family. Together, we have six adult children (Jack has two and Heather has four, including one who is estranged—the child of Heather's teen pregnancy—as well as one adopted from an overseas orphanage) and three grandchildren. We are Gen-Xers and puzzle with so many over the Millennial and Gen-Z struggles our children deal with—an alarming rate of anxiety, loneliness, and a lack of coping skills plague these two generations that have just entered adulthood or are entering it now, according to a plethora of research and statistics.

Both of us and our spouses (Bruce and Darlene; Heather and Jack), know of victory in our adult children's lives. We have celebrated their successful choices, achievements, and growth. Two of them were named class valedictorian, two others are seminary graduates, one has a PhD, two serve in ministry positions, and three others are ministry volunteers. At the time of this writing, seven are college graduates and eight are either working or full-time homemakers. We find so much joy and delight in seeing our adult children thrive and do what the Lord has called and created them to do.

But we also deeply and painfully know of failure, lack, betrayal, lies, disappointment, rejection, and loss. We know what it means to wait on God. We know what it is to keep praying when the hoped-for answers do not come. We know that broken relationships aren't always mended, and past mistakes are not always forgiven. We know that some adult children choose to blame rather than grow and accept personal responsibility for their adult emotions and decisions.

But, in all of that, we are assured that God can use the trials and challenges in our lives as parents to grow us spiritually and develop our compassion for others, our acceptance of ourselves, and our love for Him. This book is as much for us as it is for you. It does not offer a path to perfection. Please put it down if that is what you are looking for. God is not obligated to your (or our) version of a happy ending. Based on His Word, He is obligated to our good as we conform to the image of Jesus Christ. Romans 8:28-29 reminds us that good is always connected to how well each of us reflects Christ.

> We know that God causes all things to work together for good to those who love God, to those who are called according to His purpose. For those whom He foreknew, He also predestined to become conformed to the image of His Son, so that He would be the first-born among many brethren.

Therefore, these prayers are designed to help you conform to Christ more and more in your heart, mind, and actions. They are also written so that you can pray for the same on behalf of your adult children. Reflecting Jesus Christ can be summarized through the attributes of His Spirit, which we find listed for us in Galatians 5:22-23 and can be summarized as follows:

- love
- joy
- peace

- patience
- kindness
- goodness
- faithfulness
- gentleness
- self-restraint

The extent to which your own heart and your adult children's hearts reflect these qualities will determine the level of spiritual growth experienced on the journey of life. While degrees, jobs, titles, income, and the like are often what our culture looks to in order to designate success or failure, God looks to the heart. He looks to these nine attributes of His Spirit, which ought to define each of us as His adult children.

Friend, you are in good company as you read through this book and pray through these guided prayers, writing your own notes, words of gratitude, prayer needs, or answers. You are in the company of many other parents who, like us, continue to look to the Lord for help toward our own personal development and maturity as well as our adult children's. We have written this book for you with hearts full of compassion and understanding from our own lives and experiences. Parenting well in today's culture is a difficult task. It is also a role that the enemy seeks to tear down and destroy. No parent has fulfilled their role perfectly. But we can take comfort in knowing that no one is outside the reach of God's overarching grace and redemption.

Before we get into the prayers, you will find short opening reflections that mention four key parental traps. These reflections are intended to help you pray more effectively as well as free you from some painful misconceptions about our roles as parents. We have noticed that many parents with adult children are weighed down by heavy burdens that keep them in despair and defeat, and these burdens hinder their prayers and limit their joy and contentment. As you read about the parental traps so many of us fall into, our hope is that you'll come to know freedom from those traps and, as a result, experience more powerful times of prayer for your children.

We have also kept the prayers short so that you can provide your own narrative along the way, and so that we can cover as many topics as possible. If it turns out that a certain prayer doesn't apply to you and your adult children's lives, then just move on to the next one. We wanted to cover as many prayer possibilities as we could.

Dr. Bruce and Darlene Wilkinson; Atlanta, Georgia
Heather and Jack Hair; Dallas, Texas

Parental Traps

Trap One:
"If Only I Had Been a Better Parent"

The first reaction parents have when their adult child or children turn away from the Lord or get involved with a sinful lifestyle is to blame themselves. But think about it—when we do that we are blaming ourselves for another adult's poor choices. Only parents innately embrace this way of thinking. "If only I would have taught them to read the Bible better, or if only I hadn't _____, then my adult child wouldn't be making these terrible choices."

The Bible is clear about our responsibilities as parents, isn't it? As parents, we are to raise our children in the admonition of the Lord. To love and obey the Lord. To belong and serve God in a local church. To make godly decisions.

But after more than fifty years of ministry all over the world, I (Bruce) still haven't met one parent who ever said, "I parented my children perfectly. I never overreacted. I never made a mistake. I never missed praying with them every morning and night. I never missed having daily devotions with the family. I never over-disciplined or under-disciplined my children. I never sinned personally as their parent, never lied, never stole anything, never was

privately immoral with pornography or lust, never watched anything inappropriate on TV or the Internet, never became angry
with God for letting me down, never missed reading my Bible,
never missed my monthly fasts..."

Numerous of our friends were raised by alcoholic parents.
Guess what? Some of their siblings became alcoholics while their
other brothers or sisters, living in the same home, with the same
traumatic environment, chose never to drink and are living for
God. Ultimately, all the children grew into adulthood and made
their own choices. So, would those alcoholic parents only blame
themselves for their children who made poor decisions and never
embrace the joy from those adult children who made right decisions?

Other friends were married but later divorced, and some
divorced when their children were at the most vulnerable stages.
Nearly all of them are convinced today that their divorce caused
their adult children's problems. Yet, the truth is—their divorce did
have a negative impact, but some of their children overcame those
wounds and are happily married today while others have chosen
to divorce like their parents.

We have other friends who had a tragic divorce at the season
when their children were most vulnerable, yet they took extensive
steps to help their children work through this and forgive all the
hurts. Both parents continued to take responsibility to help their
children learn from the process and make right decisions. Today,
their children are all flourishing. This doesn't negate the powerful damaging impact of that broken relationship and marriage,
but ultimately, each of their children had to make their own decisions as adults.

I could go on and on, but I hope you are starting to get my
point. All of us wish that we could turn back the clock and parent again with all the wisdom we have gained over the years. But
that's not how God organized life. His timetable to have and raise

children naturally occurs when we are young. This was God's best choice and the wisest for all concerned.

A number of important factors must be overcome in order for each of us with adult children to live according to God's best and move on with joy in our lives. The first factor focuses on a three-stage forgiveness process.

The first stage of forgiveness focuses on God. If you struggle with how you parented your children, then the first stage of forgiveness is to realize that God awaits your confession of your mistakes and sins and stands ready to forgive you. If you have received Jesus Christ as your personal Savior, He stands ready to extend His full and complete forgiveness regarding your parenting.

The wise thing to do is to take the time to write on a piece of paper all of your parental failings as they come to mind, and then to ask the Lord to forgive you for each of them. Then, from that point, walk in the Lord's forgiveness. Live no more with the terrible burden of failure. As Paul said, forget those things that are behind and live in the present for the best future. Stop permitting continuous self-accusation. Live as a forgiven sinner, as all of us must choose to do.

The second stage of forgiveness focuses on your children. When the time is right, tell your children one at a time that you want to speak to them about their childhood for a few moments. Start by sharing your love for them and then say something like, "I wish I had been a better father/mother to you when you were growing up. I realize that I failed you by _____ (be specific), especially the times when _____. I take full responsibility for my mistakes and sins and humbly ask you to forgive me. Will you forgive me?"

Don't defend or excuse your previous actions, just seek your adult child's forgiveness. It's critical that you are as specific as you can be regarding the wounds of the past since unforgiveness is related to specific wounds. Don't fall into the trap of saying, "I know that I wasn't the perfect parent. Will you forgive me?" Ask forgiveness for those things that were the most painful to your children.

When you are finished and the child has forgiven you, ask this follow-up question: "I know that I forgot some other things that hurt your heart. Would you share them so I can apologize?"

You cannot overestimate the power of your adult child forgiving you! And you cannot overestimate the healing that will occur in both of your hearts. Broken relationships have been amazingly restored just through that conversation.

I remember teaching truth to an audience of more than five thousand adults and what unexpectedly occurred when I asked how many of them needed to forgive their parents. Over three thousand immediately raised their hands. You should have seen the tears followed by joy as I led them in the next hour through the forgiveness process as they forgave their parents for each of the wounds they had caused.

Then I asked how many of them needed to ask their children to forgive them, and the same number raised their hands. After they had forgiven their parents, their hearts were open to commit to go home and apologize and seek the forgiveness of their children.

The third stage of forgiveness focuses on you. The final stage of forgiveness relates to you forgiving yourself for these painful parenting mistakes or sins. Jesus died so that a holy God could forgive you for all your sins, so don't try to be more holy than God and not choose to forgive yourself. Again, the key is to forgive yourself for each of those inappropriate attitudes and actions. Extend compassion to yourself—you are worthy of forgiving yourself!

Because this is such an important topic in every person's life, I have written *The Secret of Lasting Forgiveness: How to Find Peace by Forgiving Others and Yourself.* Tens of thousands of people have also used my video course in their small groups, their churches, and their personal lives to find forgiveness: *70X7: Finding Peace by Forgiving Others and Yourself* (available at Brucewilkinsoncourses .org). I recently returned from the Philippines where I led 8,800 Christian lay leaders of discipleship groups to forgive others and themselves. The personal breakthroughs were massive and widespread. Their lives were set free through the act of genuine, heartfelt forgiveness. So can yours!

Forgiveness that is truly heartfelt radically changes our hearts and lives. The forbidding walls erected around our hearts against those who have hurt us crumble and fall to the ground. Relationships are restored with a wonderful new beginning. We finally are free again to love our children without hidden baggage or restraint. Without working through this forgiveness process, you will have a difficult time praying for your adult children with a free and clean heart. You will live with the weight of guilt and shame rather than forgiveness and freedom.

So, now it's your turn:

1. Ask the Lord to forgive you for your parental mistakes and sins.

2. Ask each of your children individually to forgive your specific acts that wounded them.

3. Forgive yourself fully for each of those acts and live in peace and freedom.

The final word on this topic is to practice the powerful principle of the apostle Paul: "...forgetting those things which are behind and reaching forward to those things which are ahead" (Philippians 3:13 NKJV). After experiencing forgiveness from God, from each of your children, and finally from yourself, then let the past be the past. Stop living in the terrible "Land of Unending Regret." Let it all go. Move on. Live free of the past and enjoy the present!

Trap Two:
"I'm Responsible for My Adult Child's
Choices and Lifestyle"

When that twenty-one-year-old man I wrote about earlier stands before the judge for selling drugs, do you think he'll blame his parents (who never took drugs) for his illegal choices? Or if he blamed his parents for what happened when he still lived in their home, do you think the judge will even permit that blame into the courtroom? Absolutely not!

That young man is now an adult, and he, not his parents, is fully and completely responsible for his own choices. No judge will permit the guilty person to blame their illegal actions on their childhood. No one would ever consider such blame thrown back to their childhood.

One of Darlene's good friends has two adult children. One is living as a responsible adult and the other just came out of a year-long prison sentence for selling drugs. And he's back in the area, still selling drugs. Which of those two adult children's decisions are to be laid at their parents' feet? Neither. Why? Each person who reaches adulthood is responsible for their own choices and actions.

Yet parents everywhere take on themselves the blame for their adult children's mistakes, illegal actions, abuses, thefts, prostitution, alcoholism, drug addictions, divorce. Why is that? Does it make sense to blame your parenting as the primary cause for the damaging choices of your adult children? If I've heard it once, I've heard it from scores of despairing parents: "If only I would have…"

This trap is devastating and, honestly, never ends. Every time one of our adult children chooses another destructive attitude or action, we have an additional reason to blame ourselves for not parenting better. We open the "blame box" once again and start playing the "blame game." No matter how hard we may try, this parental trap makes us lose every single game. Every single time. And we continue to play that treacherous game, year after year.

Think about it for a moment: This trap deceives us into believing that our adult children are locked in failure because we failed in some way as their parents. We are grabbing responsibility from them and assigning it to ourselves. Our illogical thinking concludes that our children aren't really responsible for their terrible decisions—we are! Their problems were ultimately caused by our poor parenting.

On the other hand, if our adult children are well-adjusted and flourishing, how many of us respond to their successes as if our amazing parenting were the cause of it all? In all these years, I've never heard a parent take that responsibility. Instead, they are proud of their children's choices and actions. Somehow, we slide into the misconception that our children's successes are from their own choices, and their failures are from our bad parental choices. Does that make any sense to you?

Somewhere along the line, we parents must cut the apron strings of false responsibility for the decisions of our adult children. Too many parents live in self-blame for decisions and actions that were in no way related to their parenting, often years and even decades in the past.

Does God hold parents accountable for the sins of their adult children? Absolutely not. God disciplines us if we continue to be abusive or irresponsible parents—but not for our adult children's choices and actions. When each of us stands before God and gives an account of our lives, we won't be defending our poor choices by blaming the poor choices of our parents. Everyone is held accountable for their own decisions and actions.

Therefore, stop taking responsibility for any of your adult children's decisions and actions. Although we may experience pain and disappointment by their decisions and actions, we must not ever start blaming ourselves for their decisions. We may not have been always a perfect role model, but role models do not force their attitudes or actions on their offspring. Instead, our adult children make their decisions and live their lives by their choices.

Therefore, make a clean and permanent decision right now: "I am not responsible or accountable before God or anyone else, including myself, for the attitudes and lifestyle choices of my adult children. I will not allow anyone to place blame on me for their choices, and I will not permit accusation to attack me any longer. I am fully responsible for my choices and attitudes, and they are responsible for their choices and attitudes."

We must relinquish all responsibility for our adult children's decisions, including the positive and wonderful consequences from good decisions or the negative and destructive consequences from poor ones. We must guard against relieving the negative consequences from their poor decisions or they will not learn from them. When parents still carry the guilt of previous parental insufficiencies and mistakes, they are emotionally driven to intervene and relieve those painful consequences in their children's lives. But they shouldn't.

The principle that both positive and negative actions always result in predictable consequences is among God's universal laws. God teaches us by the consequences of our behaviors.

Does this mean we should never intervene to help our adult children? Of course not. But if our intervention is driven from our guilt, then God's not behind our seeming compassion to "help them one more time." Or if our interventions occur time after time, then we are definitely interfering with the work of God in their lives.

We must offload our guilt from the past and walk in the full conviction that our adult children are fully responsible for their own lives. Isn't it about time that you fully embrace this truth? If you don't, your prayers will be tainted with self-guilt instead of a heart free to discern the real truth: Your children are fully responsible for every one of their choices, both good and bad.

Walk, then, in freedom from their responsibility. Isn't it enough to deal with the responsibility for our own lives? One person, at least, believes so, and His name is God. Why not agree with Him?

Trap Three:
"But I Raised My Children Right"

Godly parents do not guarantee godly children. Raising our children in a godly manner and within the ministry of a solid Bible-teaching church does not guarantee that they will continue in our footsteps with the Lord. Who among us doesn't wish that it did guarantee they would continue!

The Lord has granted each of us the incredible gift of freedom of choice, or, as the theologians call it, "human free will," and inherent in that gift is the potential for right choices and wrong choices. Had the Lord not granted free will, humans never could have brought full joy to their Creator.

When God created Adam and Eve, they were without sin and perfect, but they used their free will to directly disobey the Lord by eating fruit from the forbidden tree. They didn't have a fallen nature at that point. Yet they sinned. Think about this situation even deeper: God was their parent who loved them with an incalculable love. Perfect environment. Perfect parent. Perfect children. But the perfect parent witnessed the imperfect choice of major sin with terrible consequences.

Can you accept fully that we have been given by Almighty God the freedom to choose? We must embrace this reality in the lives of our children. They alone are responsible for their choices as adults, and they may choose to disobey God any time they so desire.

Just think about the next generation in the two sons of Adam and Eve: Cain and Abel. Both raised with the same parents in the same environment, yet one chose to obey and follow after God while the other chose to reject God and murder his brother. And if you read the story of Cain and his offspring, he never returned to the Lord even after God pleaded for him to choose to obey Him.

The Lord also granted you and each of your children such priceless freedom. We can never guarantee that every one of our children will choose the right path. We all have the freedom to discard the solid foundations in our lives and overthrow the good will of God for our own sinful will.

If you have adult children, you have lived long enough to witness what I'm talking about. Family, siblings, and friends—no one has a perfect record. Although all of us pray and strive to raise our children to be godly, yet they still have their freedom. So many of the last two generations (Generation X born 1965–1980 and Millennials born 1981–1996) have discarded their parents' faith, and far too many have strayed far from the Lord.

I've purposefully taken the negative side of this discussion and haven't focused on all the positive and heartwarming stories of godly adult children that I am well aware of throughout the years. I believe that most of the people who purchase this book are rooted in their pain and distress for their adult children and perhaps even grandchildren. If your adult children are flourishing personally and spiritually, then I certainly celebrate with you! But even the present situation doesn't guarantee the future choices, does it?

Just this morning I've been rereading for the umpteenth time the life stories of the godly kings of Judah recorded in 1 Kings 15–22 and 2 Kings 18–23, as well as in the related passages in 2 Chronicles. I've always found valuable insights when reflecting on these outstanding kings of Judah: Asa, Jehoshaphat, Hezekiah, and Josiah. But one thing surfaces over and over again—sometimes these godly kings had fathers who were the most ungodly, and sometimes the godliest fathers had very wicked sons. How can this be? Can't we guarantee that our godliness will automatically be transferred to our children? Sorry, but this just isn't the case, as history well records.

When you study all the nineteen kings of Israel (all wicked) and the twenty kings of Judah (eight were godly), one thing is unmistakable: Godly parents do not guarantee godly offspring, and ungodly parents do not guarantee ungodly offspring. All of us wish that God would guarantee if we raised our children in the "fear and admonition of the Lord" that all our children would choose to live a godly life. Thankfully, many do; tragically, many do not.

All of us at times wish that parenting had a written guarantee. If we as parents do X, then our children will do Y. Sometimes that formula works wonderfully, and we have much for which to thank the Lord. At other times our children reject X, reject Y, and run headstrong into the swamps of the prodigal son that Jesus taught about so eloquently.

(If you would like to understand this reality more deeply, my book *Experiencing Spiritual Breakthroughs* covers the normal path from the committed parent to the compromising child to the conflicted grandchild. Many have found this book to be enlightening and full of practical help in their quest to raise godly offspring.)

In the past ten or so years, I have seen a rebirth of the local church model for our new culture. So many contemporary churches are appealing to and reaching the new generations. I recently was asked to come and preach at a relatively new church in San Francisco composed of over two thousand Millennials. Massive numbers are coming to know Christ and are being discipled in authentic Bible study groups. The "lost generation" is flocking back to authentic Christianity.

Although some contemporary churches have unfortunately compromised biblical truth, many of them remain strong and preach the Bible openly and often for extended periods of time. When I trained those 8,800 small group leaders for four days in the Philippines, the average age was between twenty-five and forty!

One of the most powerful factors influencing our adult children is the type of church they were raised in and the type of church they select (if any) as adults. If your church isn't preaching the Bible in a clear and meaningful way, change churches. If you have pre-adult children, make sure you choose a church to their benefit, not yours—with a dynamic and meaningful children/youth/singles ministry.

Before moving to the next parental trap, I would like to underscore the importance of this trap one more time. Our three adult children are fully and completely and solely responsible for their lives. Regardless of the quality or godliness of our parenting, any one of our children is free to choose whether to follow after God or drift away from Him.

Darlene and I are not responsible for their good or poor decisions. Although we certainly celebrate their excellent choices, we equally suffer great pain if they make tragic choices against the will of God. But we don't and never will accept any responsibility for those choices.

If you have carried this terrible misconception in your heart—that you are the root cause for your adult children's sins and failures due to insufficient parenting—stop. Stop and never again embrace this lie. Anyone at any time and in any place is free to make right decisions and is free to make wrong decisions. Never again reach out and grab the responsibility for your children's decisions and actions.

I've found it very helpful to reflect even more deeply on this truth. God is our heavenly Father and intervenes in our lives as our perfect parent to help us desire the straight and narrow way. He rarely, if ever, overthrows our freedom to choose—because He honors the gift of our own choices. When we choose to disobey, He disciplines us with rebukes, chastening, and according to Hebrews 12, even with most painful scourging.

But God also reveals that any of us can harden our hearts against His love, His rebukes, His convictions, His chastening, and His scourging—and continue in sin. In other words, even our heavenly parent experiences the grief of His born-again children living in direct disobedience to Him. God never accepts responsibility for His children's choices. That's why God said, "I was crushed by their adulterous heart which has departed from Me" (Ezekiel 6:9 NKJV), and the New Testament commands us not to "grieve the Holy Spirit" (Ephesians 4:30). Why? Because our freedom to choose permits us to bring either great joy or grief to our heavenly Father.

Before leaving this chapter, I want to balance out this sobering discussion with the other side. We all know families that are incredibly loving and genuinely walk with the Lord and raise their children in the admonition of the Lord. These parents are not the "normal Christian family" but the highly committed and genuinely authentic. The parents live for the Lord openly in the marketplace, disciple their children, and raise their kids to serve the Lord in all types of situations. They are raised to love the Lord (not just attend church) and serve Him even in their young years.

The children of committed believers will 100 percent come to know Christ. Not most, not a high percentage, but all of them. You may find that statement surprising and even not want to accept it. I have made that statement to thousands of people all over the world, and then stated, "If you grew up in a truly committed Christian family and you did not become a believer, or if any of your siblings didn't become a believer, come and tell me." Not one person has ever come. Why not? Because the reality of the life of a truly committed parent is so attractive and noble and joyful, what child wouldn't want that themselves?

As those children grow into adulthood, the next question is if they will continue to walk in the ways that please the Lord. Once again, those decisions are unknown—because those adults have a free will just like Cain and Abel. In many cases, those adult children learn to stand on the shoulders of their parents and exceed their examples. In some cases, they drift down into compromise and settle for success more than service to the Lord.

Be that as it may, I often meet adults who were raised in the most unenviable circumstance but who broke from their painful past, came to know Christ, and made the decision to walk with the Lord with all their heart, soul, strength, and mind. They often make outstanding leaders due to the strength of their character and convictions.

Freedom of choice—the most wonderful and most terrible of all God's gifts to mankind. May your children, and may our children, choose to use that gift to run hard after the Lord. If not, may we continue to love them, care for them, and most of all, pray for them!

Trap Four:
"I Just Can't Stop Parenting My Adult Children"

No one ever said that parenting would be easy. And most parents assume that when their children finally finish high school and college, then their parenting responsibility will finally come to an end. What a relief! For most of the Boomer Generation (born between 1944–1964), this expectation mostly came true. But Generation Xers (1965–1980) are discovering an ever-increasing number of their children (Millennials 1981–1996) are moving back home.

This fourth parental trap is a subtle snare that captures too many parents of adult children. Although parenting continues to our death, how we parent must radically change during the seasons of our children. Obviously we parent a six-month-old infant differently than a ten-year-old or a sixteen-year-old. For most parents, these different parental seasons are transitioned naturally and quite easily. When our sixteen-year-old son yells, "Stop treating me like a child!" he's alerting us that, in his mind, we haven't made the transition quickly enough to his teenage life (whether that's true or not).

Ultimately, however, our children become our adult children. This occurs when our children leave home for college or marriage. When they leave our homes, they make their own decisions for their life. Unless we send a spy to college, we don't know what they are doing with their weekends, do we? We don't deal with their curfew or lifestyle or choices. Because we aren't aware of their choices, we don't have the basis upon which to intervene. If our adult children get married and move some distance away, we also cannot see their choices and, therefore, cannot usually intervene with our parenting style.

So much strife occurs, however, in the lives of the parents of adult children who either live nearby or move back home. The break from "parenting" our children to "mentoring" our adult children is not always an easy or quick transition for many parents.

The Bible reveals that the age of accountability was established by God when He stated to the Israelite nation—which had rebelled the final time against His will and ways—that everyone in the adult generation would wander in the wilderness for forty years and die before the nation could inherent the Promised Land. God stated that if you were twenty years old or older, you were responsible for your decision to rebel against His commands. Children who were nineteen years old or younger were excluded from His judgments as they were under their parents' decisions and were not held accountable (see Numbers 14:26-35).

The Lord also revealed that when a couple married, they were not under the authority of their parents any longer but must continue to honor them. The Bible clarifies that the new husband had an equal standing as the "head of his household" as his father did. In other words, the father and mother no longer were held responsible for either an adult (twenty years or older) or a married son or daughter.

This, then, is the basis for making the final break between the parent and the adult children. At that point, the adult children are equal to the adult parents. Both are viewed by Heaven as having full and complete autonomy and freedom of choices, attitudes, and actions.

The implications of this are vital to your life and parenting. When your children turn twenty or are married, before God they are no longer your direct responsibility as they were when they were younger. Therefore, we parents must change our parenting style, or it will displease not only our adult children, but also our heavenly Father.

We must transition as quickly as possible from "final authority" to "loving mentor." If we are wise, we hold our tongues until our adult children raise an issue and ask for our opinion. Our opinion may be accepted with gratitude or summarily dismissed. That choice is not ours but our children's.

If our children seek to move back home, we must have a clear heart-to-heart regarding the rules under which they live in our household—including the time when they commit to move out of our home. What breeds conflict and codependency is when parents don't discuss the household rules for their adult children while they live in their home.

Ultimately, all parents seek the best for their children—including their independent life, separate from the purview of their parents. They must make it on their own unless there are special conditions such as physical or psychological limitations.

We've discovered that unless parents officially make the break from parenting to mentoring, both the parents and the adult children suffer. This damages the relationship and the hearts of both parties, often hindering their prayers. Bitterness and rebellion can surface and eventually breed the desire for vengeance—and directly hinder the blessings of God.

If you need to have "the conversation" with your adult children, first discuss the issues with your spouse. Then hold a family council to clear the air, offer any needed apologies, and establish mutually agreed upon household standards. Although life will likely bring some challenges along the way, these can surely be negotiated, or the adult children may need to be asked to leave. Hopefully that will never happen to you, but one of our acquaintances even had the police come and force their adult child to leave the premises. The son would not stop selling drugs from his basement apartment in his parents' home.

No matter what you may be facing with your adult children, God stands ready to hear and respond to your prayers and relieve your burdens. Heather Hair and I are both parents of adult children, both with numerous grandchildren, and we hope that the *Prayers of Blessing over My Adult Children* will be a major boost to your prayers and release many wonderful and liberating answered prayers from the throne room of God.

Take your time and begin praying at least one prayer each day for your adult children, and then go back through them again. The Lord has some wonderful answers awaiting your prayers! We join with you in hopeful anticipation of what the Lord will do in your own life and in the lives of your adult children as you seek His heart and His will, for His glory.

How to Use This Book

Are you ready to start using your power of prayer more fully in the lives of your adult children? It starts with you. Praying for yourself as a parent will shape your relationship with your adult children the way you hope to. We've come alongside to help you do just that.

Here are some suggestions on how to use this book. We've included sixty-five guided prayers and affirming truths to reflect on. You can choose the one or ones you feel most relate to your needs as a parent or your adult child's needs and pray it repeatedly for a number of days. Or you can move progressively through the book, picking a new prayer every day. Don't make it a big task, just read and then pray.

You can also skim through the sixty-five prayers and affirming truths to give you a mindset-boost on framing your own prayers, using your own thoughts and desires to prompt you. It's totally your call. We just know the power of prayer and how critical prayer is in shaping lives.

We've divided this guided prayer book into five sections. The first section contains prayers formed around the concepts presented in the "parental traps" section of the book. We have provided prayers and Scripture passages for each of the four parental traps. Then there are additional sections that will guide you in praying the truths of God's Word for your adult children, praying through specific struggles as well as for present and future victories, and praying for the character qualities of Jesus Christ to be made manifest in your adult children's lives. Again, please keep in mind that some of the prayers might not apply to you or your adult child.

Along the way, we have provided headings that will enable you to find the prayers that apply to you and your adult children. Please note that we have deliberately chosen to focus on the more difficult issues faced by parents. If your adult children are successful and your relationship with them is strong and you want to pray them on to even greater successes, this book isn't intended for you. This book has been written more as a guide for those who are struggling with their adult children and have little left to give outside of prayer.

Even if your situation appears dim, remember, you do not need to pray as if you are losing the battle. When you do that, Satan has already won. Jesus secured our victory over every demonic and evil injection into our lives on earth, so praying with the mindset already secure in His victory will help you and your adult children live out the victory that is rightfully yours in Him.

In summary, in the remainder of this book you'll find:

> Section One: Praying Through the Traps
>
> Section Two: Praying in the Truth
>
> Section Three: Praying Through the Struggles
>
> Section Four: Praying for the Victories
>
> Section Five: Praying for the Character of Christ
>
> Appendix: Scripture Passages to Reflect On or Pray
> Regarding Parenting and Prayer

Keep in mind that guided prayers are not magical words to make all your hopes come true. But they can help you focus your prayers on what is often the overlooked root of spiritual issues we face. Remember, the main thing in having your prayers answered is found in your abiding relationship with Jesus Christ. But it is also our hope that these prayers will help you zero in on more specific, regular, and affirming prayers for yourself and your family members. We pray as your prayer journey continues to develop more fully that God Himself will bless you with a supernatural covering and motivation to pray regularly, fervently, and with great expectations!

Section One:

Praying Through the Traps

Parental Trap #1:

"If Only I Had Been a Better Parent"

Prayer One

If we confess our sins, He is faithful and righteous to forgive us our sins and cleanse us from all unrighteousness (1 John 1:9).

Lord, You know as well as I know how many parental mistakes and sins I committed over the years. I admit that I have made wrong choices that have affected my children in a negative and painful way. I wasn't always present. I didn't always walk in a spirit of peace. I was selfish, narrow-minded, and even judgmental. Lord, I have no excuse for these mistakes and sins. Blaming my own childhood, parents, or some trauma in my life will only continue the cycle of pain. No matter what happened to me, all blame for my parental mistakes and sins belongs to me because these were my choices. And I chose poorly far too many times. Forgive me, Lord. In Jesus' name, amen.

I am grateful for _____

_____

Notes _____

_____

Prayer Needs _____

_____

Answered Prayer _____

_____

Prayer Two

> I pray that the eyes of your heart may be enlightened,
> so that you will know what is the hope of His calling,
> what are the riches of the glory of His inheritance in
> the saints (Ephesians 1:18).

Lord, I ask that You enlighten my adult children's minds in such a way that will allow them to forgive me for the parental mistakes and sins I have committed against them. Open their hearts to a greater desire to love and forgive me and their other parent (or parents) as well. I do not want to see my adult children living with regret, bitterness, or hatred in their hearts due to anything I have done or that I failed to do—or due to anything their other parent(s) did or did not do but should have done. Set my adult children free through forgiveness. In Jesus' name, amen.

I am grateful for _____

_____

Notes _____

_____

Prayer Needs _____

_____

Answered Prayer _____

_____

Prayer Three

He rescued us from the domain of darkness, and transferred us to the kingdom of His beloved Son, in whom
we have redemption, the forgiveness of sins (Colossians 1:13-14).

L ord, help me not get lost in the question of what would be
different had I been a better parent. Help me not rehearse the
what-ifs over and over until my spirit is so low and my self-love
is so lost that I am no good to You, myself, or anyone else. I cannot change the past. I cannot fix the past. I cannot undo the past.
Blaming, doubting, and questioning what I did or didn't do as a
parent does not help the present, and it certainly does not help
the future. Please help me to let those thoughts go. Help me to
release them. Help me to rest in the truth that You have enough
strength and enough power to redeem the mistakes of the past and
restore whatever has been lost or broken. When I spend my precious thoughts worried about the past, I am dishonoring You and
Your power to overcome it. Forgive me and free me from damaging thoughts rooted in the past. In Jesus' name, amen.

I am grateful for _____

_____

Notes _____

_____

Prayer Needs _____

_____

Answered Prayer _____

_____

Prayer Four

He made Him who knew no sin to be sin on our
behalf, so that we might become the righteousness of
God in Him (2 Corinthians 5:21).

Lord, free me from guilt. Free me from comparison. Free me
from the bonds of wishing I had done better, knowing I
should have done better and feeling not good enough. God, I have
failed as a parent in certain areas and at specific times. Had I the
wisdom and maturity that I have now, I may have acted or reacted
differently. I may have made wiser choices. But I didn't. And I have
to live with that reality. Denying that truth does not help me, and
it does not help my adult children. Help me be honest with myself,
with You, and with my adult children. Free me from pretense. Free
me from perfectionism. Help me lift the shield of faith, knowing
that Your forgiveness and grace can cover all. In Jesus' name, amen.

I am grateful for _____

_____

Notes _____

_____

Prayer Needs _____

_____

Answered Prayer _____

_____

Prayer Five

Each one should test their own actions. Then they can take pride in themselves alone, without comparing themselves to someone else, for each one should carry their own load (Galatians 6:4-5).

Lord, sometimes I worry about what other people think. I want to look, in their eyes, like I was a great parent. I see so many parents posting on social media or I see them at church, and it looks like they have it all together—their smiling faces, their perfect poses. It makes me feel like what I did wasn't good enough. I didn't give enough. Or I didn't do enough. I ask You to release me from the chains of comparison. Help me to see behind the veil so that I am not deceived into thinking that pictures on social media reflect reality as we often think they do. We are all flawed humans. We all make mistakes. And parenting isn't a race or competition, either. I am responsible to run only my own race, with You as my judge. Help me know where to look for hope—in You. In Jesus' name, amen.

I am grateful for _____

_____

Notes _____

_____

Prayer Needs _____

_____

Answered Prayer _____

_____

Prayer Six

I, even I, am the one who wipes out your transgressions for My own sake, and I will not remember your sins (Isaiah 43:25).

Lord, I want to forgive myself for the pain I have caused my adult children—whether when they were younger or older. I need to forgive myself for not living up to my expectations or my children's expectations. Your love for me on the cross was sufficient for all my sins. Yet if I hold on to blame and judgment against myself, I am negating the power of Your sacrifice. Your sacrifice is enough for me, so, in faith, I choose to forgive myself for my failures and sins as a parent. Help me, Lord, to continue to forgive myself and release myself from self-blame in the days ahead. In Jesus' name, amen.

I am grateful for _____

_____

Notes _____

_____

Prayer Needs _____

_____

Answered Prayer _____

_____

Prayer Seven

> If you are presenting your offering at the altar, and
> there remember that your brother has something
> against you, leave your offering there before the altar
> and go; first be reconciled to your brother, and then
> come and present your offering (Matthew 5:23-24).

Lord, give me the courage I need to apologize to my adult children
and to ask their forgiveness for the ways that I have hurt them.
Give me the wisdom and insight I need to specifically identify
these ways so that I can address them and ask for forgiveness. Prepare my children's hearts to receive my apology and request for forgiveness as well, please. I admit that doing this causes me anxiety
and fear. I ask for Your calming peace to overwhelm me so that I
can do what my adult children need in order for them to live freely
in a spirit of forgiveness toward me. In Jesus' name, amen.

I am grateful for _____

_____

Notes _____

_____

Prayer Needs _____

_____

Answered Prayer _____

_____

Prayer Eight

In everything give thanks; for this is God's will for you
in Christ Jesus (1 Thessalonians 5:18).

Lord, rather than dwell on the "if onlys" of life, I want to take this time to thank You for the things I did right. I want to give You praise for seeing me through my own growth, maturity, and development as a parent. I honor You for Your loving care, which showed me grace in the midst of the personal struggles I faced. While my kids were growing up, I was naïve on a lot of levels. But You developed and grew me each day. Thank You, Lord, for never giving up on me. Help me to recognize the good I did and to show myself grace for the ways I did not parent as I think I should have. I love You and praise You, Lord, and I am grateful for all the parenting successes and precious moments You allowed me to experience—as well as the wisdom You gave me along the way. In Jesus' name, amen.

I am grateful for _____

_____

Notes _____

_____

Prayer Needs _____

_____

Answered Prayer _____

_____

Parental Trap #2:

"I'm Responsible for My Adult Child's Choices and Lifestyle"

Prayer One

Above all, keep loving one another earnestly, since love
covers a multitude of sins (1 Peter 4:8).

Lord, help me to offload my guilt from the past in order to walk
in the full conviction that my adult children are fully responsible for their own lives. Help me to fully embrace this truth. I
do not want my prayers to be tainted any more with self-guilt
rather than a heart that is free to discern the truth. The truth is
that my adult children are fully responsible for every one of their
choices, both good and bad. Release me from the lies that tell me I
am responsible. They made their choices and ought to accept and
live out the full consequences of those choices in order to learn
life's valuable lessons about love, compassion, gratitude, and more.
Thank You for showing me this and giving me this wisdom. In
Jesus' name, amen.

I am grateful for _____

_____

Notes _____

_____

Prayer Needs _____

_____

Answered Prayer _____

_____

Prayer Two

Love covers all transgressions (Proverbs 10:12).

Lord, my adult children are free to make their own choices. They are free to turn to the light or walk in the darkness. They have free will. This free will is Your intention, a gift given by You in order to reveal truth to them through lessons learned. I ask You to help me relinquish all responsibility for my adult children's decisions, including the good and the bad. I ought not to take their positive and wonderful results in life as my own. Neither should I take the negative and destructive consequences as my own fault either. Help me guard against relieving the negative consequences from their decisions, preventing them from having the opportunity to learn from them. Allow me to release my adult children into the space necessary to learn and grow, even if it is difficult to witness and watch. In Jesus' name, amen.

I am grateful for _____

_____

Notes _____

_____

Prayer Needs _____

_____

Answered Prayer _____

_____

Prayer Three

Concerning this I implored the Lord three times that it might leave me. And He has said to me, "My grace is sufficient for you, for power is perfected in weakness." Most gladly, therefore, I will rather boast about my weaknesses, so that the power of Christ may dwell in me (2 Corinthians 12:8-9).

Lord, help me to cut the apron strings of false responsibility for the decisions of my adult children. I release self-blame and exchange it for Your assurance of grace. It can be difficult to do that, though, when my adult children, or others, cast blame my way. Whether it's in talking to other family members or posting about toxic parents or bio-family members—it seems like a lot of blame is coming my way from my adult children. Lord, help me not reflect the collective conscience of this generation of adult children, which seems to blame their parents well into adulthood for anything and everything. Help my adult children to wake up in their own hearts and minds and stop leaning on the crutch of blame and shame toward me or us as parents. In Jesus' name, amen.

I am grateful for _____

_____

Notes _____

_____

Prayer Needs _____

_____

Answered Prayer _____

_____

Prayer Four

Each one of us will give an account of himself to God
(Romans 14:12).

Lord, remind me today that You do not hold me accountable
for the sins of my adult children. When I stand before You
to give an account for my life, I won't be defending my adult children's poor choices. Each person is held accountable for their own
actions and decisions. Help me to stop feeling and believing that I
am responsible for my adult children's decisions and actions. Help
me to stop fearing their next move or their next wrong choice. Set
me free from dread. Break the chains of guilt. Release me from feelings of personal responsibility toward those who are old enough
to make their own choices, however poor those choices may be.
Allow me the peace that comes from prayer and faith. Let Your
peace and rest set deeply into my soul, revealing the truth of the
passage that says Your peace passes even understanding. In Jesus'
name, amen.

I am grateful for _____

Notes _____

Prayer Needs _____

Answered Prayer _____

Prayer Five

Accept one another, just as Christ also accepted us to
the glory of God (Romans 15:7).

Lord, help me to close the "blame box" and stop playing the
"blame game." Help other family members to do the same
as well. There are no winners in that game. This trap deceives all
of us into believing that our adult children are locked into failure
because we failed as parents in some way. It is stealing their own
God-given personal responsibility and assuming it's ours. Please
help me to root out this damaging misconception of blame. Give
me wisdom to understand that being responsible means to have
the capacity for moral decisions and therefore to be answerable
or accountable for one's actions—to act on the basis of one's own
preferences and choices. My adult children are responsible for their
actions. Help them to see that as well, and to stop blaming me (or
others) for any failures on their part. In Jesus' name, amen.

I am grateful for _____

_____

Notes _____

_____

Prayer Needs _____

_____

Answered Prayer _____

_____

Prayer Six

Your hands made me and fashioned me; give me understanding, that I may learn Your commandments (Psalm 119:73).

Lord, guard me against relieving the negative consequences my adult children have walked into by choosing darkness over light. Help me to release myself from parental insufficiencies. Had I been more mature, I may have made different choices, but I cannot change where I was in my own growth and development as a parent. So, Lord, help me to allow my adult children to mature as quickly as possible by restraining myself from removing the consequences of their wrong choices. My adult children are free to turn to the light or to turn to the darkness. They are free to follow You or to follow their own fleshly desires. They are free to make their own choices. Help my adult children to grow and learn from their choices. Keep them from the destructive and unhealthy pattern of blaming their parents, or others, for choices they personally make. In Jesus' name, amen.

I am grateful for _____

_____

Notes _____

_____

Prayer Needs _____

_____

Answered Prayer _____

_____

Prayer Seven

> I acknowledged my sin to You, and my iniquity I did not hide; I said, "I will confess my transgressions to the LORD"; and You forgave the guilt of my sin (Psalm 32:5).

Lord, I know that positive and negative actions always produce predictable consequences and that You teach us and mature us by the consequences of our behaviors. Because of this truth, I want to be sure that whenever I do reach out to help my adult children, I am not doing so in a spirit of guilt. If I interfere out of a heart of guilt, I am interfering with Your work in their lives. Help me to walk in the full conviction that my adult children are fully responsible for their own lives. Help me to embrace this truth. Help me to believe this truth. In Your Word there was a man who asked You to help his unbelief. I ask the same of You today. Help me to believe Your truth that my adult children are responsible for every one of their choices, both good and bad. In Jesus' name, amen.

I am grateful for _____

_____

Notes _____

_____

Prayer Needs _____

_____

Answered Prayer _____

_____

Prayer Eight

I can do all things through Him who strengthens me
(Philippians 4:13).

Lord, I give You praise for growing and maturing me specifically
in this area of my life. Thank You for opening my eyes to see
that it is not I who needs to receive the blame for the mistakes
of my adult children. Even if they, or someone else, sends it my
way, I praise You that You have shown me that it is not mine to
own. Thank You for setting me free. Thank You for showing me
how to let go of guilt and shame and replace them with an abso-
lute trust in Your plan. I want to honor You by walking strong in
the power of Your love and choosing to love myself in this season
of life, even when the temptation arises to blame myself for things
that are not mine to own. Give me wisdom and insight to overcome and resist such temptation and surround me with a shield of
protection through the love of Christ that will extinguish, in faith,
the fiery darts of accusation that the enemy seeks to aim my way.
May these fiery darts be quenched before they reach my heart or
soul, and may I walk in joy, peace, and gratitude each day. In Jesus'
name, amen.

I am grateful for _____

_____

Notes _____

_____

Prayer Needs _____

_____

Answered Prayer _____

_____

Parental Trap #3:

"But I Raised My Children Right"

Prayer One

God demonstrates His own love toward us, in that while we were yet sinners, Christ died for us (Romans 5:8).

Lord, raising my children in a godly manner does not guarantee they will continue in the pathway that pursues You. You have granted each of us the freedom of choice, also known as free will. Inherent in that gift is the potential for right choices and wrong choices. Even though I believe that the foundation I provided while they were growing up gave my adult children what they needed in order to make mature, adult decisions, it is no guarantee. You made Adam and Eve without sin and placed them in an environment uncontaminated by sin. And yet they chose to follow Satan's leading, and they and their descendants suffered the consequences. Help me not to blame You, God, for those times when I fall into the trap of believing I did everything right and yet somehow You allowed my children to go on the wrong path. In Jesus' name, amen.

I am grateful for _____

_____

Notes _____

_____

Prayer Needs _____

_____

Answered Prayer _____

_____

Prayer Two

All have sinned and fall short of the glory of God (Romans 3:23).

Lord, help me to fully accept that You have given each of us free choice and free will. We all have the freedom to choose our actions, reactions, emotions, and responses in word or deed. My adult children are alone responsible for their choices. The good foundation that I provided for them does not guarantee that they will make good choices as an adult. Each person is different. Each path is different. There are other elements and environments that affect what people do. Adult choices are not solely determined on parental upbringing. There are social influencers. Peer influencers. Internal spiritual and personality battles and discoveries. Lord, I know that no one goes through life perfectly. And just because I raised my children to believe in You does not guarantee that they will. I release their choices and belief systems to You to nurture and mature. In Jesus' name, amen.

I am grateful for _____

_____

Notes _____

_____

Prayer Needs _____

_____

Answered Prayer _____

_____

Prayer Three

> Do you see a man wise in his own eyes? There is more
> hope for a fool than for him (Proverbs 26:12).

L ord, Your Word gives us so many examples of ungodly parents
whose adult children turned out to be godly. There are also
examples of godly parents whose adult children turned out to be
ungodly. Thank You for giving us these examples as a way of teaching
us that our parenting does not set in stone the actions and
choices, and even the beliefs, of our children once they are grown.
We cannot demand faith, love, and purity. We can only encourage
them. We cannot command commitment, responsibility, and
respect. We can only model and nurture them or discipline toward
their aim. But once our children are adults, we have no control
over what they do, say, or think. Thank You for reminding me in
Your Scripture that I cannot guarantee that godliness will automatically
be transferred to my children or grandchildren. History
proves otherwise. Godly parents do not ensure godly offspring.
Ungodly parents do not guarantee ungodly offspring. I praise You
for reminding me of this today. In Jesus' name, amen.

I am grateful for _____

_____

Notes _____

_____

Prayer Needs _____

_____

Answered Prayer _____

_____

Prayer Four

The steadfast of mind You will keep in perfect peace,
because he trusts in You (Isaiah 26:3).

Lord, it pains me when my adult children make poor choices. Of course I celebrate when they make good choices, but bearing the grief of their tragic choices becomes more than I can bear at times. When my adult children go against Your will and do not value themselves by their actions or words, it breaks my heart. I am not the root cause for their sins and failures. I refuse to embrace this lie, God. Help me to gain wisdom on how to deal with and process my own grief and sorrow over their failures as adults. Also, help me to gain wisdom on how to celebrate their good choices in a way that doesn't lend itself to comparison between children or pride on my part. I ask for Your help, Lord, because the grief I feel when my adult children continue on a path of sin is such a weight. Give me joy in place of sorrow. Give me peace in place of worry. Fill me with faith in place of guilt. And keep me from blaming their other parent or their siblings for the poor choices my adult children make. In Jesus' name, amen.

I am grateful for _____

_____

Notes _____

_____

Prayer Needs _____

_____

Answered Prayer _____

_____

Prayer Five

> Brethren, I do not regard myself as having laid hold of
> it yet; but one thing I do: forgetting what lies behind
> and reaching forward to what lies ahead, I press on
> toward the goal for the prize of the upward call of God
> in Christ Jesus (Philippians 3:13-14).

Lord, You are our heavenly Father. You intervene in all of our lives as our perfect parent to help us desire and live out the path of wisdom. I know that You do not overthrow our freedom to choose, and it must break Your heart to see wrong or poor choices. That is why You discipline us with rebukes, chastening, and even pain. You want us all to learn how to make wise choices in life. I know that despite our best efforts as parents, anyone can harden their heart against You. Anyone can turn a deaf ear to Your chastening and convictions. Even You, as a perfect parent, experience the grief of Your children turning from You. Free will means just that—free will. You never accept responsibility for Your children's choices when they go against You. Neither should I accept responsibility for my adult children's choices. They are free to choose as they do, and then live with the results of those choices. In Jesus' name, amen.

I am grateful for _____

_____

Notes _____

_____

Prayer Needs _____

_____

Answered Prayer _____

_____

Prayer Six

Indeed, there is not a righteous man on earth who continually does good and who never sins (Ecclesiastes 7:20).

L ord, for me to fall into the "but I raised my children right" trap, I must first ignore or deny any mistakes and sins I did commit as a parent. I was not a perfect parent. I may have loved my children fully, but in my own growth and development, I made mistakes along the way. Lord, forgive me for claiming, if only to myself, that I raised my children right, therefore my adult children should not do anything wrong. Forgive me for failing to see my own shortcomings and sins in their upbringing. Forgive me for failing to ask for their forgiveness for things that may have hurt them or hindered their personal growth and maturity. In Jesus' name, amen.

I am grateful for _____

_____

Notes _____

_____

Prayer Needs _____

_____

Answered Prayer _____

_____

Prayer Seven

Having been justified by faith, we have peace with
God through our Lord Jesus Christ (Romans 5:1).

Lord, I wish I could push the reset button and have a do-over
in some areas of parenting. Maybe doing everything that I
thought was right in my own eyes wasn't the best thing for them. I
don't know. I know that I tried to give them every opportunity to
succeed, but somehow, I fell short. Forgive me for these ongoing
feelings of regret mixed with pride. My pride is a defensive mech-
anism so that I won't feel like I failed. But God, truth be told, I
am not perfect. You know that. And I should know that too. Help
me to forgive myself for how my adult children are now behaving.
Help me to show myself grace rather than seek to cover up what
I'm feeling by invoking a spirit of pride. In Jesus' name, amen.

I am grateful for _____

_____

Notes _____

_____

Prayer Needs _____

_____

Answered Prayer _____

_____

Prayer Eight

Everyone who exalts himself will be humbled, and he
who humbles himself will be exalted (Luke 14:11).

L ord, thank You for delivering me from this trap that leads
to pride and self-defensiveness. I give You praise that You saw
fit to give me wisdom and insight enough to realize that I did not
do everything right. But even if I did most things right, I need to
realize that each person has his or her own free will. What I did to
raise my children in the right way may or may not be received by
them. They are each their own individual, and they will choose the
path they decide to walk. I honor You, God, for setting me free
from this trap and allowing me the ability to enjoy my life and this
empty-nest season with all the satisfaction of knowing that ultimately, You are in control of all things. I am under You, and You
are over all. I love You and give You praise. In Jesus' name, amen.

I am grateful for _____

_____

Notes _____

_____

Prayer Needs _____

_____

Answered Prayer _____

_____

Parental Trap #4:

"I Just Can't Stop Parenting My Adult Children"

Prayer One

Set your mind on the things above, not on the things
that are on earth (Colossians 3:2).

Lord, children become adults. That's how You formed things to
be. Our children do not remain dependent children forever.
There comes a time when they are to leave home and provide for
themselves. When they do, or even if they are still living as adults
in our home, they make their own decisions for their lives. They
make their own choices, good or bad. While we can seek to influence those choices to be good, we cannot control them. Help me
release the lie that I can, or should, control their actions. I cannot.
I should not. In doing so, I am preventing their own growth and
maturity through learning about life. Help me to transition from
parenting my child to mentoring my adult child. It is not an easy
or quick transition, but I want to cooperate with You in making
the transition. Show me where I am combatting this transition
rather than embracing it. In Jesus' name, amen.

I am grateful for _____

_____

Notes _____

_____

Prayer Needs _____

_____

Answered Prayer _____

_____

Prayer Two

Children, obey your parents in the Lord, for this is right. HONOR YOUR FATHER AND MOTHER (which is the first commandment with a promise), SO THAT IT MAY BE WELL WITH YOU, AND THAT YOU MAY LIVE LONG ON THE EARTH. Fathers, do not provoke your children to anger, but bring them up in the discipline and instruction of the Lord (Ephesians 6:2-3).

Lord, Your Word says that when children are older, they are still to honor their parents. When I negate or counteract that honor by parenting my adult child, I am keeping them from fully embracing Your will for their lives. Help me to give space for them to honor me. Help me to step back and allow them to discover the power of honor and respect. Help me to draw up healthy boundaries that do not allow for dishonor or disrespect, or for being used by my adult children. Help me not hold on to the notion that I want to be their friend so much that I am unwilling to require honor and respect from them. In Jesus' name, amen.

I am grateful for _____

_____

Notes _____

_____

Prayer Needs _____

_____

Answered Prayer _____

_____

Prayer Three

We know that God causes all things to work together
for good to those who love God, to those who are
called according to His purpose. For those whom He
foreknew, He also predestined to become conformed
to the image of His Son, so that He would be the first-
born among many brethren (Romans 8:28-29).

L ord, help me to transition in my own thinking from "final
authority" to "loving mentor" in my adult children's lives.
Help me to hold my tongue until my adult children raise an issue
and ask for my opinion. Give me restraint and self-respect so that
I don't keep doting on them or telling them what to do. Show me
how to give an opinion and then be okay if they do not agree with
or follow my opinion. The choice is theirs. It is not mine. Help
me also to establish any rules for when my adult children choose
to live or stay in my home. Help me not to fear conflict or hurting
their feelings to such a degree that I do not voice what the healthy
rules and boundaries are for behavior in my home. In Jesus' name,
amen.

I am grateful for _____

_____

Notes _____

_____

Prayer Needs _____

_____

Answered Prayer _____

_____

Prayer Four

If the Son makes you free, you will be free indeed (John 8:36).

Lord, help me to admit I made mistakes. Help me to own up to my personal failings. Help me to stop trying to fix the past by still parenting in the present—when parenting is no longer my role. I have to accept the truth that I did not do all things well. My adult children did not turn out in all matters the way I had hoped. I feel guilty, God, but You have asked me to forgive others and myself. You have placed my guilt at the cross. My adult children still blame me for their problems, so I try to fix their problems to make the blame stop. God, this is not helping anything at all. Help me let go, forgive myself, and move on. In Jesus' name, amen.

I am grateful for _____

_____

Notes _____

_____

Prayer Needs _____

_____

Answered Prayer _____

_____

Prayer Five

If any of you lacks wisdom, let him ask of God, who gives to all generously and without reproach, and it will be given to him (James 1:5).

L ord, give me insight to understand what is appropriate and what is not. Give me wisdom to know where I need to establish boundaries. Lord, so many adult children disrespect us as parents on social media and talk about setting boundaries against us, but then they want us to do everything for them. I would never allow an adult to talk badly about me and then want me to give them something on the very next day. Let me understand how much I deserve to be respected for my role. Yes, I made mistakes. Yes, I was not perfect. But when I continue to parent my adult children, I am merely perpetuating their own lack of growth. Help me to understand this and let go. In Jesus' name, amen.

I am grateful for _____

_____

Notes _____

_____

Prayer Needs _____

_____

Answered Prayer _____

_____

Prayer Six

You are still fleshly. For since there is jealousy and strife among you, are you not fleshly, and are you not walking like mere men? (1 Corinthians 3:3).

Lord, help me to stop comparing my family to other people's families. Help me to stop comparing my adult kids to other people's adult kids. Free me from the trap of social media where people tend to post only the best, most favorable updates and photos. Free me from the comparison trap, Lord. Show me how to let go and be at peace with how my adult children are choosing to live their lives now. Help me not to feel the need to continue parenting them in order to get them to the point I want them to be, or to have grandchildren for my benefit, or any other thing. Show me the importance of releasing them into adulthood as they are. In Jesus' name, amen.

I am grateful for _____

_____

Notes _____

_____

Prayer Needs _____

_____

Answered Prayer _____

_____

Prayer Seven

Be devoted to one another in brotherly love; give pref-
erence to one another in honor (Romans 12:10).

L ord, whatever career my adult children choose or pursue is their
doing. Help me not pressure them to pursue certain careers or
to stay at one they do not prefer. Show me how to be content with
the life path they have chosen. I want to be free from my desire
to get them to a certain point by a certain age, in their housing
and family and career. This is their life to live. Let me honor their
choices. Let me honor their actions. Let me honor their inactions.
In doing so, I will be giving them the space they need to discover
what path they want to pursue the most. And I will be removing
the burden of pleasing me, if they are carrying that burden. In
Jesus' name, amen.

I am grateful for _____

_____

Notes _____

_____

Prayer Needs _____

_____

Answered Prayer _____

_____

Prayer Eight

Peace I leave with you; My peace I give to you; not as
the world gives do I give to you. Do not let your heart
be troubled, nor let it be fearful (John 14:27).

Lord, thank You for the power of self-restraint. Thank You for
giving me the opportunity to grow in this area of my life,
and for revealing to me the abundant wisdom of letting go and
allowing others to make their own decisions. I give You praise and
honor for how You have matured me and are continuing to do so.
Though it is not easy for me to watch my adult children have to
learn their own lessons in life, it is freeing to know that You love
them as much as I do. In fact, Your love for them surpasses my own.
I can trust that You have important things for them to do and are
using this time and these lessons to develop their hearts toward
You. Help my adult children to learn quickly so that they can also
experience the power of peace in You. I give You all praise, honor,
and glory in Christ Jesus' name—amen.

I am grateful for _____

_____

Notes _____

_____

Prayer Needs _____

_____

Answered Prayer _____

_____

Section Two:

Praying
in the Truth

Truth One:
Belief Brings Answers

Prayer One

I say to you, all things for which you pray and ask, believe that you have received them, and they will be granted you (Mark 11:24).

Lord, Your Word makes it clear that all things for which I pray and ask, if I believe that I have received them, will be granted to me. Faith the size of a mustard seed is enough for You to move mountains on my behalf. Lord, I want to believe this to be true. Help my unbelief. Help me to pray bold prayers of faith on behalf of my adult children. When doubt creeps in, remind me of Mark 11:24. In Jesus' name, amen.

I am grateful for _____

_____

Notes _____

_____

Prayer Needs _____

_____

Answered Prayer _____

_____

Truth Two:
You Are Free from Condemnation

Prayer Two

There is now no condemnation for those who are in
Christ Jesus (Romans 8:1).

Lord, when things don't go as planned, it is easy to blame myself
or to blame others. I have made mistakes and have failed as a
parent in a number of ways. But I know, according to Romans 8:1,
that You do not stand with Your finger pointed at me while judg-
ing and condemning me. You know my path. You know what life
influences shaped me in such a way to make the mistakes I did.
While I am sorry for my past failures, I ask that You remove the
personal guilt or even the external guilt and blame that others cast
my way. Also, Lord, please let my adult children know and rest in
Your selfless, uncondemning love as well. Let them know they are
truly loved and accepted by You. In Jesus' name, amen.

I am grateful for _____

_____

Notes _____

_____

Prayer Needs _____

_____

Answered Prayer _____

_____

Truth Three:
God Has Great Plans for Your Family

Prayer Three

"I know the plans that I have for you," declares the
LORD, "plans for welfare and not for calamity to give
you a future and a hope" (Jeremiah 29:11).

Lord, thank You for the good plans You have for me and for my
family. Thank You for the truth of Your Word, which tells us
about these good plans. I rest my worry and dread on the reality
of Your loving care. Take it from me. Take my anxious thoughts
from me. Take my adult children's uncertainty about the future
from them as well. Remind us in Your own personal ways that You
have a good future planned for us as a family and for each of us as
individuals. Help us to give You our hearts in trust and anticipation of the good things You have in store up ahead. In Jesus' name,
amen.

I am grateful for _____

_____

Notes _____

_____

Prayer Needs _____

_____

Answered Prayer _____

_____

Truth Six:
God Hears Prayers

Prayer Six

The eyes of the LORD are toward the righteous and His
ears are *open* to their cry (Psalm 34:15).

Lord, thank You for the confidence You have given to me that
when I pray to You, covered in the righteousness of Jesus
Christ, You hear my prayers and my cries. I do not have to won-
der whether You hear me. I am assured, through Your Word, that
because of the righteousness I have through Your Son Jesus Christ,
my Savior, I am heard. Please hear these prayers for my adult children at this time. Respond in the way You know is best. Help my
adult children seek the pathway to growth, happiness, and spiritual maturity. Thank You for Your faithfulness. In Jesus' name,
amen.

I am grateful for _____

Notes _____

Prayer Needs _____

Answered Prayer _____

Truth Seven:
God Answers Prayers According to His Compassion

Prayer Seven

O my God, incline Your ear and hear! Open Your eyes
and see our desolations and the city which is called by
Your name; for we are not presenting our supplications
before You on account of any merits of our own, but
on account of Your great compassion (Daniel 9:18).

Lord, thank You that You do not answer my prayers based on my
own merits, but rather, You answer them based on the compassion You possess and show through Jesus Christ. I can boldly
approach Your throne of grace, knowing that I am made complete
in Christ. My prayers are able to reach the highest heavens due to
His saving power and grace, which He secured for me on the cross.
Help my adult children to know Christ more fully. Give them
the boldness to pray to You—a boldness that is rightfully theirs
through Christ as well. In Jesus' name, amen.

I am grateful for _____

_____

Notes _____

_____

Prayer Needs _____

_____

Answered Prayer _____

_____

Truth Eight:
God Gives All Good Things

Prayer Eight

Every good thing given and every perfect gift is from above, coming down from the Father of lights, with whom there is no variation or shifting shadow (James 1:17).

Lord, remind me today of all of the good things You provide. It's easy to get lost in the loss, regret, blame, or confusion. I don't want my prayers to focus only on the lack or pain. Remind me that all good things come from You. Show me the good things to focus on. Shift my view from my disappointments as a parent to my hope in You. Let me see the good You have provided and the good You will provide when I put my trust in You. You have *good* planned for my adult children. Usher this good into their reality, Lord. In Jesus' name, amen.

I am grateful for _____

_____

Notes _____

_____

Prayer Needs _____

_____

Answered Prayer _____

_____

Section Three:

Praying Through the Struggles

Struggle One:
Blame

Prayer One

As far as the east is from the west, so far has He removed
our transgressions from us (Psalm 103:12).

Lord, I ask that You set my adult children free from the chains
of blame. Help them to see the need for personal ownership of
their choices and decisions. Give them eyes to see that no one was
raised in a perfect home by perfect parents. Neither was I. None of
us were. Please remove toxic people from my adult children's lives
who want to focus on blaming others for their issues. Lord, show
my adult children the way out of this sin called blame so they can
find the freedom of love and forgiveness. In Jesus' name, amen.

I am grateful for _____

_____

Notes _____

_____

Prayer Needs _____

_____

Answered Prayer _____

_____

Struggle Two: Irresponsibility

Prayer Two

If you are wise, you are wise for yourself, and if you scoff, you alone will bear it (Proverbs 9:12).

L ord, I pray for my adult child right now that he or she will live with full responsibility over what needs to be done. May they live in such a way that they are able to hold a full-time job, show up to work as needed, pay their bills on time, and relate to other people in a respectful manner. May they have the determination and responsibility to volunteer to help others in whatever way You have designed them to be of service to the world at large and the body of Christ. I ask that You will show them how to be resourceful and that You will remove from their lives any enabling relationships that are making it difficult for them to accept full responsibility. In Jesus' name, amen.

I am grateful for _____

_____

Notes _____

_____

Prayer Needs _____

_____

Answered Prayer _____

_____

Struggle Three: Indecision

Prayer Three

Delight yourself in the LORD; and He will give you the desires of your heart (Psalm 37:4).

Lord, I ask for Your supernatural power to infuse a strong will within my adult children to such a degree that decisions can be made soundly. Give my adult child the ability to trust his or her own judgment and to allow for mistakes. Help my adult child to understand that not all decisions will be the right decisions but that mistakes allow us the opportunity to learn, develop, and grow. Help my adult child identify their true wants and desires as well. Give him or her wisdom to understand the difference between societal or peer pressure and their own likes and dislikes. Let them find freedom in being themselves and rest in the awareness that decisions are there to be made, learned from, and used to move life forward. In Jesus' name, amen.

I am grateful for _____

_____

Notes _____

_____

Prayer Needs _____

_____

Answered Prayer _____

_____

Struggle Four:
Anxiety

Prayer Four

...casting all your anxiety on Him, because He cares for you (1 Peter 5:7).

L ord, I pray against any anxiety that plagues my adult child or children. Whether it is social anxiety or professional anxiety or even personal anxiety, I ask that You set my adult child free from the crippling hold of fear. Fear does not originate from You. Fear is a reflection of Satan himself. I ask that You remove any demonic or satanic influences from my adult child's life that are being used to stoke the embers of anxiety in his or her soul. In Jesus' name, amen.

I am grateful for _____

_____

Notes _____

_____

Prayer Needs _____

_____

Answered Prayer _____

_____

Struggle Five:
Lack of Commitment

Prayer Five

Let your statement be, "Yes, yes" or "No, no"; anything
beyond these is of evil (Matthew 5:37).

Lord, I ask that You reveal to my adult child the importance of
commitment. Whether it is commitment to his or her own
moral values, a friendship, a job, schooling, or the pursuit of a
dream or goal—whatever it is, I ask that You enforce and reinforce
the proper need for commitment in his or her life. Where my adult
child has learned that commitment is lacking in others, help them
to accept personal responsibility to do better than what has been
modeled for them. Help them avoid the trap of pointing out the
faults of others in order to remain in a spirit of a lack of commitment themselves. In Jesus' name, amen.

I am grateful for _____

_____

Notes _____

_____

Prayer Needs _____

_____

Answered Prayer _____

_____

Struggle Six:
Spiritual Relationship

Prayer Six

Abide in Me, and I in you. As the branch cannot bear
fruit of itself unless it abides in the vine, so neither can
you unless you abide in Me (John 15:4).

Lord, will You give my adult child a heart for You? Will You light
the fire for spiritual awareness, knowledge, and relationship
with You? I ask that You surround my adult child with people who
have a vibrant, growing relationship with You and allow those relationships to provide a positive example of spiritual maturity. Let
my adult child experience Your love, peace, and grace firsthand.
Let them smile in Your joy. Show them Your purpose for their life.
In Jesus' name, amen.

I am grateful for _____

_____

Notes _____

_____

Prayer Needs _____

_____

Answered Prayer _____

_____

Struggle Seven:
Dishonor

Prayer Seven

Do nothing from selfishness or empty conceit, but
with humility of mind regard one another as more
important than yourselves (Philippians 2:3).

Lord, I ask that You remove any spirit or action of dishonor that
still exists in my adult child. If my adult child has broken off
his or her relationship with me as a parent, I ask that You send the
Rebuker to remove the demonic influence driving them from obeying Your command of honor. Honoring parents is the only command
that comes with a promise, and I want my adult child to experience
the promise You have for them when they choose to honor us as parents. Help my adult child to honor others in words and actions as
well, whether it's friends, posts on social media, coworkers, a boss,
church members, the pastor, or anyone they meet along life's journey. Let my adult child be known as a person of honor, even honoring himself or herself through the decisions they make regarding
their body, time, money, and pursuits. In Jesus' name, amen.

I am grateful for _____

_____

Notes _____

_____

Prayer Needs _____

_____

Answered Prayer _____

_____

Struggle Eight: Perfectionism

Prayer Eight

The Law was given through Moses; grace and truth were realized through Jesus Christ (John 1:17).

Lord, free my adult child from the bond of perfectionism. Help my adult child to cut themselves some slack. Help them not to hold others to a perfect standard either. Teach grace. Teach giving the benefit of the doubt. Teach that mistakes happen. Teach my adult child to understand that perfectionism strangles the life out of every pursuit. Set my adult child free to explore his or her interests, career, and relationships based on grace and love. In Jesus' name, amen.

I am grateful for _____

_____

Notes _____

_____

Prayer Needs _____

_____

Answered Prayer _____

_____

Section Four:

Praying
for the Victories

Victory One:
Contentment

Prayer One

I know how to get along with humble means, and I also know how to live in prosperity; in any and every circumstance I have learned the secret of being filled and going hungry, both of having abundance and suffering need. I can do all things through Him who strengthens me (Philippians 4:12-13).

Lord, contentment is often learned through the challenges life brings our way. It's difficult to learn in a culture and society that seeks to make us discontent, always wanting more, always pointing out the grass that grows greener on the other side. I ask for Your grace in teaching this wonderful gift to my adult children. Show them they are enough. Show them they have enough. Show them how to be at rest in much or little. Help them to focus on what they have rather than on what they do not have. Help them to honor and embrace the relationships they have rather than compare themselves to others. Teach them contentment so that they can be at peace each day and bring peace to those around them. In Jesus' name, amen.

I am grateful for _____
_____

Notes _____
_____

Prayer Needs _____
_____

Answered Prayer _____
_____

Victory Two:
Spiritual Intimacy

Prayer Two

As the deer pants for the water brooks, so my soul
pants for You, O God. My soul thirsts for God, for
the living God; when shall I come and appear before
God? (Psalm 42:1-2).

L ord, I ask that You burn the flame brightly within the hearts of
my adult children so that they will desire a close, abiding relationship with You. I ask for wisdom for them as they seek You in
Your Word. I ask for enlightenment for them as they ponder Your
truth. Lord, lead my adult children to the church home that will
nurture them and foster an atmosphere for spiritual intimacy to
develop. Thank You for drawing my adult children into a closer
relationship with You. In Jesus' name, amen.

I am grateful for _____

_____

Notes _____

_____

Prayer Needs _____

_____

Answered Prayer _____

_____

Victory Three: Spiritual Service

Prayer Three

As each one has received a special gift, employ it in serving one another as good stewards of the manifold grace of God (1 Peter 4:10).

Lord, I pray that You will reveal to my adult children the ways they can serve You. Whether it is through a paid position or a volunteer role, may they reflect You as they go throughout their everyday lives, and may they understand that spiritual service is vital. Show them ways to be a magnet of Your love to others. Help them to be spiritual servants within their own homes, workplace, and in their relationships. Reveal to them the special gifts You have given to them for serving You and enable them to develop these gifts for even greater purposes. In Jesus' name, amen.

I am grateful for _____

_____

Notes _____

_____

Prayer Needs _____

_____

Answered Prayer _____

_____

Victory Four: Stewardship

Prayer Four

His master said to him, "Well done, good and faithful slave. You were faithful with a few things, I will put you in charge of many things; enter into the joy of your master" (Matthew 25:21).

Lord, I ask You to help my adult children be wise stewards of their time, talents, and treasures. Place them under spiritual teachers who will give them insight into how to live as kingdom stewards. Show them the power of wisely managing what You have entrusted to them. Give them an eternal view of life so that they do not get caught up in the race of storing up for themselves treasures on earth that will eventually rot. Help me also to be a wise steward so that I can be an example to my adult children of what biblical stewardship looks like. In Jesus' name, amen.

I am grateful for _____

_____

Notes _____

_____

Prayer Needs _____

_____

Answered Prayer _____

_____

Victory Five:
Relational Health

Prayer Five

The whole Law is fulfilled in one word, in the statement, "YOU SHALL LOVE YOUR NEIGHBOR AS YOURSELF" (Galatians 5:14).

L ord, I pray that my adult children will experience healthy, mature relationships with their friends, co-workers, and family members. Please bless them with people who are respectful, kind, and loving. Place a hedge of protection around them to guard them against entering into relationships with people who are toxic or will bring them emotional or spiritual harm. I ask that You will heal any wounds or insecurities my adult children have so that they are more likely to be drawn to emotionally mature people in their relationships. Affirm to them their value and Your love for them. Help them to draw the line against any type of abusive, manipulative, or damaging behavior that comes from others. In Jesus' name, amen.

I am grateful for _____

_____

Notes _____

_____

Prayer Needs _____

_____

Answered Prayer _____

_____

Victory Six:
Personal Grace

Prayer Six

See to it that no one comes short of the grace of God;
that no root of bitterness springing up causes trouble,
and by it many be defiled (Hebrews 12:15).

Lord, I ask that You enable my adult children to show themselves grace. Your grace is a powerful life force that breathes hope into our hearts. But when we fail to show ourselves grace for our own failings or mistakes or flaws, we fall into the trap Satan has set up to keep us in bondage to his lies. Help my adult children to know and fully believe they are whole and loved in Your eyes. When they fail, equip them to own up to their failures and then show themselves grace so they can move on. Release them from the captivity of comparison or unrealistic expectations. Give them a zest for life that will enable them to fully live out Your calling and purpose for them in every way. In Jesus' name, amen.

I am grateful for _____

_____

Notes _____

_____

Prayer Needs _____

_____

Answered Prayer _____

_____

Victory Seven: Forgiveness

Prayer Seven

Let all bitterness and wrath and anger and clamor and slander be put away from you, along with all malice. Be kind to one another, tender-hearted, forgiving each other, just as God in Christ also has forgiven you (Ephesians 4:31-32).

Lord, I pray for Your extra measure of grace and mercy to be poured out into the hearts of my adult children. Let no root of bitterness strangle them in any way. Give them the gift of knowing how to forgive others and themselves. Show them the importance of forgiveness. Walk them through the process of forgiving. Release them from anger and deliver them from bitterness. Show them the power of letting go of past hurts and holding on to Your hope. Help me not to provoke my adult children in any way toward anger. When they behave poorly toward me or hurt me, give me the spiritual wisdom to restrain from reacting wrongly. Provide the space needed for forgiveness to flourish in my heart and in my adult children's hearts as well. In Jesus' name, amen.

I am grateful for _____

_____

Notes _____

_____

Prayer Needs _____

_____

Answered Prayer _____

_____

Victory Eight:
Emotional Healing

Prayer Eight

After you have suffered for a little while, the God of all grace, who called you to His eternal glory in Christ, will Himself perfect, confirm, strengthen and establish you (1 Peter 5:10).

Lord, I pray for Your supernatural power to heal my adult children from any emotional wounds they have experienced. Whether these wounds came from me, themselves, or anyone else is not the point. I ask for complete and total healing for all emotional wounds that my adult children struggle with and are bound by. Set them free to fully live out Your purpose in their lives—a purpose filled with love, joy, and peace. Show them where they are wounded so that they will know where they need healing. Help me to be authentic in my prayers for them and my relating to them so that I can be of help to them. Show me what I need to say and do to help them heal. Show them what they need to do as well, and give them the courage to move toward that goal. In Jesus' name, amen.

I am grateful for _____

_____

Notes _____

_____

Prayer Needs _____

_____

Answered Prayer _____

_____

Section Five:

Praying for the Character of Christ

Character One:
Love

Prayer One

Now faith, hope, love, abide these three; but the greatest of these is love (1 Corinthians 13:13).

L ord, I ask that You will fill my adult children with Your love so much so that it overflows from them to others. Remind them to take time to abide in You, Jesus. Let Your Holy Spirit be their ever-present companion. Let love rule their choices and thoughts. I ask for their future or current spouse to be filled with godly love as well. Let the words and actions of my adult children be selfless, humble, nonprovoking, and life-giving in every way. I pray that You will surround my adult children with others who demonstrate godly love so they will see it modeled regularly. In Jesus' name, amen.

I am grateful for _____

_____

Notes _____

_____

Prayer Needs _____

_____

Answered Prayer _____

_____

Character Two:
Joy

Prayer Two

Now may the God of hope fill you with all joy and
peace in believing, so that you will abound in hope by
the power of the Holy Spirit (Romans 15:13).

Lord, I long to see my adult children filled with joy. It is by the
power of Your Holy Spirit that You can bring this about.
Keep them from the pains and discouragements sent by the enemy
to defeat them. Show them the pathway of life and joy, which is
in You and is found in a pursuit of Your presence and Your Word.
Lead my adult children to seek You in all things. Let them know
the joy that comes from Your closeness and Your faithfulness to
walk with them each step of life's journey. Open doors for them
that will lead to greater joy, life, and happiness, and give them the
courage to walk through those doors. In Jesus' name, amen.

I am grateful for _____

_____

Notes _____

_____

Prayer Needs _____

_____

Answered Prayer _____

_____

Character Three:
Peace

Prayer Three

Let the peace of Christ rule in your hearts, to which
indeed you were called in one body; and be thankful
(Colossians 3:15).

L ord, peace is the prize. You have called each of us to live in peace
as one body, and to be thankful. I ask that You will develop
this virtue of peace in my adult children's hearts and minds. Show
them the benefits that come from knowing peace. Let them have
the wisdom to understand the importance of not only seeking
peace for their own lives but preserving it with others. Peace
reflects the character of Christ like little else because it demonstrates confidence and calm amidst life's stormy circumstances. It
communicates trust and faith in You. Thank You for making the
gift of peace available to us, and help my adult children to pursue
and cultivate it in their lives. In Jesus' name, amen.

I am grateful for _____

_____

Notes _____

_____

Prayer Needs _____

_____

Answered Prayer _____

_____

Character Four:
Patience

Prayer Four

If we hope for what we do not see, with perseverance we wait eagerly for it (Romans 8:25).

Lord, patience can save a lot of heartache. When we learn to be patient, we find it much easier to let go and allow You to be in control. I ask that You give my adult children the wisdom to know and embrace this virtue of patience. Give them lessons that enable them to learn the art and skill of patience. Let Your Holy Spirit be so full within them that patience becomes a natural response to life's challenges. In Jesus' name, amen.

I am grateful for _____

_____

Notes _____

_____

Prayer Needs _____

_____

Answered Prayer _____

_____

Character Five: Kindness

Prayer Five

She opens her mouth in wisdom, and the teaching of kindness is on her tongue (Proverbs 31:26).

Lord, let kindness fill the hearts of my adult children. May kindness be on their tongues and affect their actions. Demonstrate to them the importance of kindness in their relationships and even toward themselves. Show them the power of kindness. I ask that Your Holy Spirit inspire them to spread kindness through all their thoughts and actions. Convict my adult children when they are not being kind. Convict their heart before they let an unkind word come from their mouth. Surround them with people who are also kind so that they can benefit from this great spiritual gift. In Jesus' name, amen.

I am grateful for _____

_____

Notes _____

_____

Prayer Needs _____

_____

Answered Prayer _____

_____

Character Six:
Goodness

Prayer Six

While we have opportunity, let us do good to all people, and especially to those who are of the household of the faith (Galatians 6:10).

Lord, I ask that You help my adult children to grow in such a way that the virtue of goodness permeates all they say and do. Show them how spending time with You and in Your Word matures these qualities within them. Give my adult children a heart of goodness not only for those they can help but also for themselves, their family members, and their co-workers. Let good flourish in and around them and overflow to those they meet. Let them shine the light of Your love, faithfulness, and goodness so that they help brighten a dark world. In Jesus' name, amen.

I am grateful for _____

_____

Notes _____

_____

Prayer Needs _____

_____

Answered Prayer _____

_____

Character Seven:
Faithfulness

Prayer Seven

Let love and faithfulness never leave you; bind them around your neck, write them on the tablet of your heart (Proverbs 3:3 NIV).

Lord, write faithfulness on the tablet of my adult children's hearts. Let it guide and direct them in all they do. Give them a circle of relationships with people who will also be faithful to them so that they may be protected from the pains of betrayal and abandonment. Show my adult children the value of faithfulness and in keeping their word. May they experience, with the help of Your Spirit, the power and purity of faithfulness. And may they learn from Your own faithfulness to them how they can show this important character trait to others. In Jesus' name, amen.

I am grateful for _____

_____

Notes _____

_____

Prayer Needs _____

_____

Answered Prayer _____

_____

Character Eight:
Gentleness

Prayer Eight

Let your gentleness be evident to all. The Lord is near
(Philippians 4:5).

Lord, I ask that my adult children recognize the value of showing gentleness to all. Let them be known for their strength coupled with gentleness. In courage, give grace. In confidence, give humility. In power, give peace. When these are coupled together, gentleness is the result. I pray for a spirit of meekness to come through in what my adult children say and do. May their gentleness serve as a reflection of Your grace and kindness. Convict them of any hostility, rage, or destructive behavior or thoughts so that they can repent and pursue Your Spirit's presence and gentleness in their lives. In Jesus' name, amen.

I am grateful for _____

_____

Notes _____

_____

Prayer Needs _____

_____

Answered Prayer _____

_____

Character Nine:
Self-Restraint

Prayer Nine

The Spirit God gave us does not make us timid, but
gives us power, love and self-discipline (2 Timothy 1:7).

Lord, I pray for my adult children to exercise diligence and
demonstrate self-restraint in every area of life. I ask for Your
supernatural power...to enable them to keep from running up debt
by buying more than they can afford. To preserve their bodies and
health by refraining from using substances that could harm them.
To give them the wisdom to withdraw from worry's strangling grip
over their thoughts. To help them spend their time in ways that
please You. Help my adult children to honor You by practicing
self-restraint and thus resembling the character of Christ in every
way. In Jesus' name, amen.

I am grateful for _____

_____

Notes _____

_____

Prayer Needs _____

_____

Answered Prayer _____

_____

those of his household, he has denied the faith and is worse than an unbeliever.

Proverbs 22:15

Foolishness is bound up in the heart of a child;
The rod of discipline will remove it far from him.

Psalm 103:13

Just as a father has compassion on his children,
So the LORD has compassion on those who fear Him.

2 Corinthians 12:14

Here for this third time I am ready to come to you, and I will not be a burden to you; for I do not seek what is yours, but you; for children are not responsible to save up for their parents, but parents for their children.

Proverbs 23:13-14

Do not hold back discipline from the child,
Although you strike him with the rod, he will not die.
You shall strike him with the rod
And rescue his soul from Sheol.

1 Timothy 3:4

He must be one who manages his own household well, keeping his children under control with all dignity.

Proverbs 10:1

The proverbs of Solomon.
A wise son makes a glad father,
But a foolish son is a grief to his mother.

Appendix

Scripture Passages to Reflect On or Pray Regarding Parenting and Prayer

Ephesians 6:1-4

Children, obey your parents in the Lord, for this is right. HONOR YOUR FATHER AND MOTHER (which is the first commandment with a promise), SO THAT IT MAY BE WELL WITH YOU, AND THAT YOU MAY LIVE LONG ON THE EARTH. Fathers, do not provoke your children to anger, but bring them up in the discipline and instruction of the Lord.

Proverbs 22:6

Train up a child in the way he should go,
Even when he is old he will not depart from it.

Proverbs 13:24

He who withholds his rod hates his son,   .
But he who loves him disciplines him diligently.

Joshua 4:20-24

Those twelve stones which they had taken from the Jordan, Joshua set up at Gilgal. He said to the sons of Israel, "When your children ask their fathers in time to come, saying, 'What are these stones?' then you shall inform your children, saying, 'Israel crossed this Jordan on dry ground.' For the Lord your God dried up the waters of the Jordan before you until you had crossed, just as the Lord your God had done to the Red Sea, which He dried up before us until we had crossed; that all the peoples of the earth may know that the hand of the Lord is mighty, so that you may fear the Lord your God forever."

Psalm 127:3

Behold, children are a gift of the Lord, the fruit of the womb is a reward.

Titus 2:7

...in all things show yourself to be an example of good deeds, with purity in doctrine, dignified...

Proverbs 29:15

The rod and reproof give wisdom,
But a child who gets his own way brings shame
to his mother.

Proverbs 29:17

Correct your son, and he will give you comfort;
He will also delight your soul.

Deuteronomy 6:6-9

"These words, which I am commanding you today, shall be on your heart. You shall teach them diligently to your sons and shall talk of them when you sit in your house and when you walk by the way and when you lie down and when you rise up. You shall bind them as a sign on your hand and they shall be as frontals on your forehead. You shall write them on the doorposts of your house and on your gates."

Proverbs 1:8-9

Hear, my son, your father's instruction
And do not forsake your mother's teaching;
Indeed, they are a graceful wreath to your head
And ornaments about your neck.

Proverbs 19:18

Discipline your son while there is hope, and do not desire his death.

1 Peter 5:3

...nor yet as lording it over those allotted to your charge, but proving to be examples to the flock.

Exodus 20:12

"Honor your father and your mother, that your days may be prolonged in the land which the Lord your God gives you."

Hebrews 12:7-11

It is for discipline that you endure; God deals with you as with sons; for what son is there whom his father does not discipline? But if you are without discipline, of which all have become partakers, then you are illegitimate children and not sons. Furthermore, we had earthly fathers to discipline us, and we respected them; shall we not much rather be subject to the Father of spirits, and live? For they disciplined us for a short time as seemed best to them, but He disciplines us for our good, so that we may share His holiness. All discipline for the moment seems not to be joyful, but sorrowful; yet to those who have been trained by it, afterwards it yields the peaceful fruit of righteousness.

1 Timothy 5:8

But if anyone does not provide for his own, and especially

Deuteronomy 11:19 (ESV)

"You shall teach them to your children, talking of them when you are sitting in your house, and when you are walking by the way, and when you lie down, and when you rise."

Titus 2:4 (ESV)

...and so train the young women to love their husbands and children...

Proverbs 23:22

Listen to your father who begot you,
And do not despise your mother when she is old.

Colossians 3:20

Children, be obedient to your parents in all things, for this is well-pleasing to the Lord.

Psalm 78:4

We will not conceal them from their children,
But tell to the generation to come the praises
of the LORD,
And His strength and His wondrous works that
He has done.

Psalm 127:3-5

Behold, children are a gift of the LORD,
The fruit of the womb is a reward.
Like arrows in the hand of a warrior,
So are the children of one's youth.
How blessed is the man whose quiver is full of them;
They will not be ashamed
When they speak with their enemies in the gate.

Hebrews 12:11

For the moment all discipline seems painful rather than pleasant, but later it yields the peaceful fruit of righteousness to those who have been trained by it.

Deuteronomy 4:9 (ESV)

"Only take care, and keep your soul diligently, lest you forget the things that your eyes have seen, and lest they depart from your heart all the days of your life. Make them known to your children and your children's children..."

1 Peter 4:8 (ESV)

Above all, keep loving one another earnestly, since love covers a multitude of sins.

Proverbs 19:18-19

Discipline your son while there is hope,
And do not desire his death.
A man of great anger will bear the penalty,
For if you rescue him, you will only have to
    do it again.

Colossians 3:20-21

Children, be obedient to your parents in all things, for this is well-pleasing to the Lord. Fathers, do not exasperate your children, so that they will not lose heart.

Psalm 119:1

How blessed are those whose way is blameless,
Who walk in the law of the LORD.

Deuteronomy 6:4-5

"Hear, O Israel! The LORD is our God, the LORD is one! You

shall love the LORD your God with all your heart and with all your soul and with all your might."

Luke 1:17

"It is he who will go as a forerunner before Him in the spirit and power of Elijah, TO TURN THE HEARTS OF THE FATHERS BACK TO THE CHILDREN, and the disobedient to the attitude of the righteous, so as to make ready a people prepared for the Lord."

1 John 1:9

If we confess our sins, He is faithful and righteous to forgive us our sins and to cleanse us from all unrighteousness.

Deuteronomy 4:10

"Remember the day you stood before the LORD your God at Horeb, when the LORD said to me, 'Assemble the people to Me, that I may let them hear My words so they may learn to fear Me all the days they live on the earth, and that they may teach their children.'"

Acts 2:38-39

Peter said to them, "Repent, and each of you be baptized in the name of Jesus Christ for the forgiveness of your sins; and you will receive the gift of the Holy Spirit. For the promise is for you and your children and for all who are far off, as many as the Lord our God will call to Himself."

Proverbs 3:11-12

My son, do not reject the discipline of the LORD
Or loathe His reproof,
For whom the LORD loves He reproves,
Even as a father corrects the son in whom he delights.

Psalm 23:1-6

The LORD is my shepherd,
I shall not want.
He makes me lie down in green pastures;
He leads me beside quiet waters.
He restores my soul;
He guides me in the paths of righteousness
For His name's sake.
Even though I walk through the valley of the shadow
    of death,
I fear no evil, for You are with me;
Your rod and Your staff, they comfort me.
You prepare a table before me in the presence
    of my enemies;
You have anointed my head with oil;
My cup overflows.
Surely goodness and lovingkindness will follow me
    all the days of my life,
And I will dwell in the house of the LORD forever.

Deuteronomy 21:18-21

If any man has a stubborn and rebellious son who will not obey his father or his mother, and when they chastise him, he will not even listen to them, then his father and mother shall seize him, and bring him out to the elders of his city at the gateway of his hometown. They shall say to the elders of his city, "This son of ours is stubborn and rebellious, he will not obey us, he is a glutton and a drunkard." Then all the men of his city shall stone him to death; so you shall remove the evil from your midst, and all Israel will hear of it and fear.

1 Peter 5:5-7

You younger men, likewise, be subject to your elders; and all of you, clothe yourselves with humility toward one another, for GOD IS OPPOSED TO THE PROUD, BUT GIVES GRACE TO THE HUMBLE. Therefore humble yourselves under the mighty hand of God, that He may exalt you at the proper time, casting all your anxiety on Him, because He cares for you.

Mark 9:42

Whoever causes one of these little ones who believe to stumble, it would be better for him if, with a heavy millstone hung around his neck, he had been cast into the sea.

Joel 1:3

Tell your sons about it,
And let your sons tell their sons,
And their sons the next generation.

Deuteronomy 6:7

You shall teach them diligently to your sons and shall talk of them when you sit in your house and when you walk by the way and when you lie down and when you rise up.

2 Timothy 3:16-17

All Scripture is inspired by God and profitable for teaching, for reproof, for correction, for training in righteousness; so that the man of God may be adequate, equipped for every good work.

Ephesians 5:21

Be subject to one another in the fear of Christ.

Matthew 6:34

"So do not worry about tomorrow; for tomorrow will care for itself. Each day has enough trouble of its own."

Genesis 18:19

"For I have chosen him, so that he may command his children and his household after him to keep the way of the LORD by doing righteousness and justice, so that the LORD may bring upon Abraham what He has spoken about him."

Isaiah 38:19

"It is the living who give thanks to You, as I do today;
A father tells his sons about Your faithfulness."

Deuteronomy 5:16

"Honor your father and your mother, as the LORD your God has commanded you, that your days may be prolonged and that it may go well with you on the land which the LORD your God gives you."

Titus 1:6

...namely, if any man is above reproach, the husband of one wife, having children who believe, not accused of dissipation or rebellion.

Lamentations 3:22-23

The LORD's lovingkindnesses indeed never cease,
For His compassions never fail.
They are new every morning;
Great is Your faithfulness.

Leviticus 19:3

"Every one of you shall reverence his mother and his father, and you shall keep My sabbaths; I am the LORD your God."

Exodus 21:15

"He who strikes his father or his mother shall surely be put to death."

Exodus 10:2

"...and that you may tell in the hearing of your son, and of your grandson, how I made a mockery of the Egyptians and how I performed My signs among them, that you may know that I am the LORD."

Genesis 48:15

He blessed Joseph, and said, "The God before whom my fathers Abraham and Isaac walked, the God who has been my shepherd all my life to this day..."

Hebrews 12:7

It is for discipline that you endure; God deals with you as with sons; for what son is there whom his father does not discipline?

Hebrews 12:4-5

You have not yet resisted to the point of shedding blood in your striving against sin; and you have forgotten the exhortation which is addressed to you as sons,

"MY SON, DO NOT REGARD LIGHTLY THE DISCIPLINE
    OF THE LORD,
NOR FAINT WHEN YOU ARE REPROVED BY HIM..."

Hebrews 11:20

By faith Isaac blessed Jacob and Esau, even regarding things to come.

Ephesians 4:29

Let no unwholesome word proceed from your mouth, but only

such a word as is good for edification according to the need of the moment, so that it will give grace to those who hear.

Matthew 19:13-14

Then some children were brought to Him so that He might lay His hands on them and pray; and the disciples rebuked them. But Jesus said, "Let the children alone, and do not hinder them from coming to Me; for the kingdom of heaven belongs to such as these."

Hebrews 12:10

For they disciplined us for a short time as seemed best to them, but He disciplines us for our good, so that we may share His holiness.

Proverbs 23:24

The father of the righteous will greatly rejoice,
And he who sires a wise son will be glad in him.

Job 42:15

In all the land no women were found so fair as Job's daughters; and their father gave them inheritance among their brothers.

2 Timothy 3:15

...and that from childhood you have known the sacred writings which are able to give you the wisdom that leads to salvation through faith which is in Christ Jesus.

Psalm 127:4

Like arrows in the hand of a warrior, so are the children of one's youth.

1 Samuel 3:13

"For I have told him that I am about to judge his house forever for the iniquity which he knew, because his sons brought a curse on themselves and he did not rebuke them."

2 Timothy 3:2

For men will be lovers of self, lovers of money, boastful, arrogant, revilers, disobedient to parents, ungrateful, unholy...

1 Timothy 5:3-4

Honor widows who are widows indeed; but if any widow has children or grandchildren, they must first learn to practice piety in regard to their own family and to make some return to their parents; for this is acceptable in the sight of God.

Malachi 4:5-6

"Behold, I am going to send you Elijah the prophet before the coming of the great and terrible day of the LORD. He will restore the hearts of the fathers to their children and the hearts of the children to their fathers, so that I will not come and smite the land with a curse."

Proverbs 3:5-6

Trust in the LORD with all your heart
And do not lean on your own understanding.
In all your ways acknowledge Him,
And He will make your paths straight.

2 Samuel 12:16

David therefore inquired of God for the child; and David fasted and went and lay all night on the ground.

Genesis 17:18

And Abraham said to God, "Oh that Ishmael might live before You!"

Mark 5:22-23

One of the synagogue officials named Jairus came up, and on seeing Him, fell at His feet and implored Him earnestly, saying, "My little daughter is at the point of death; please come and lay Your hands on her, so that she will get well and live."

John 3:16-17

"For God so loved the world, that He gave His only begotten Son, that whoever believes in Him shall not perish, but have eternal life. For God did not send the Son into the world to judge the world, but that the world might be saved through Him."

Matthew 18:10

"See that you do not despise one of these little ones, for I say to you that their angels in heaven continually see the face of My Father who is in heaven."

1 Timothy 3:12

Deacons must be husbands of only one wife, and good managers of their children and their own households.

Psalm 119:9

How can a young man keep his way pure?
By keeping it according to Your word.

Philippians 4:6-7

Be anxious for nothing, but in everything by prayer and supplication with thanksgiving let your requests be made known to God. And the peace of God, which surpasses all comprehension, will guard your hearts and your minds in Christ Jesus.

Other Great
Harvest House Reading by
Bruce Wilkinson and Heather Hair

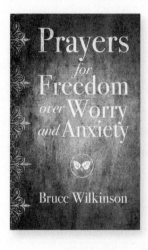

Prayers for Freedom Over Worry and Anxiety

No matter what's making you feel anxious, God cares!

Set your heart free as you are encouraged by God's truth and empowered by His love. Be uplifted as you read short devotions to quiet your mind, scripture to guide your thoughts, and prayers to help you convey your burdens to the Lord. Burdens such as...

- staying safe
- navigating your finances
- repairing relationships
- maintaining good health
- facing the future

Are you ready to release your worries and receive God's infinite peace? This book will help you in your daily prayer time, enhancing your current experience and freeing you to fully embrace heavenly peace.

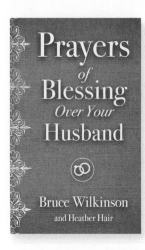

Prayers of Blessing Over Your Husband

Are you unsure of how to best pray for your husband? Do you struggle to find words that are meaningful and honest?

Prayer is one of the most beautiful gifts you can give your spouse, but trying to know his heart and pray with intention can feel overwhelming. You can't understand his every spiritual need—but God knows.

This book of insightful, guided prayers and carefully matched scriptures will enable you to pray for your husband with resolve and passion. Each day, your confidence will grow as you are inspired to approach God with a sincere and courageous heart for your spouse.

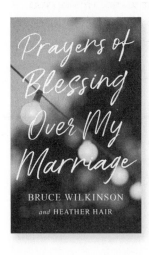

Prayers of Blessing Over My Marriage

Do you feel as though you are going through the motions in your marriage? Is your relationship feeling a bit frayed at the edges?

Prayer is one of the most powerful tools God has given us to change ourselves and our relationships from the inside out—which is why it's the best resource we can possibly turn to for revitalizing a marriage.

Bestselling author Bruce Wilkinson brings you this book of guided prayers for seeking God's blessings upon your marriage. As you pray in specific ways for your relationship, you'll experience new joys, and your confidence will grow as you see God's daily provision abound for you and your spouse.

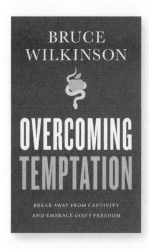

Overcoming Temptation

You believe there is hope for successfully combating temptation and the choices and habits that leave you feeling ashamed and fearful of the consequences. But you are unsure how to begin fighting back.

Victory is indeed within reach when you rely on God's grace and strength. The principles and prayers in this book, inspired and guided by powerful Scripture verses, will help you effectively war against temptation and walk in the freedom God offers every day and in every situation. You will learn the reasons we so easily succumb to temptation, and how God stands ready to intervene so you can succeed and overcome.

When you find yourself in a bad place—or even when you *think* you will be fine—seek the Lord and pray. This book will get you started with biblical tools and reminders that show how God can guide you safely through your daily battles.

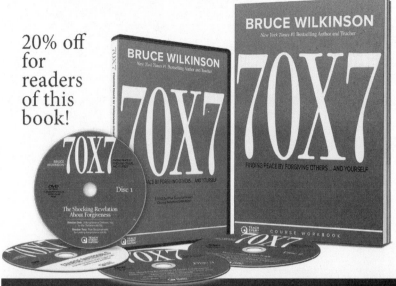